Learning foreign languages from authentic texts: theory and practice

David Little
Seán Devitt
David Singleton

Authentik
in association with CILT

ISBN 0 948003 03 0

Foreword

Ten years ago the idea of a communicative approach to language teaching was still a novelty. Some teachers seized on it eagerly, seeing in it an opportunity to give new purpose to their classes and new impetus to their pupils. Others received it with scepticism, doubting whether it could really succeed where other much-vaunted approaches and methods had so manifestly failed. Nowadays major victories are claimed for the communicative approach in every area of language teaching, and it is a rare teacher who will declare him- or herself to be anti-communicative.

The communicative approach has no single source and certainly exists in no single version. Inevitably, in the process of transmission the principles which provide its underpinning have often been diluted and sometimes been lost sight of; and many language teachers who claim to follow the communicative approach in their classroom would find it difficult to explain exactly what it consists of. Such has been the success of the missionaries who some fifteen years ago set out to convert the language teaching world to the communicative approach that in perhaps the majority of language classrooms it is manifested at least in the form of two lowest common denominators: emphasis on the spoken language and use of authentic texts. Often, however, these two phenomena are almost wholly divorced from one another in methodology and in the way classes are structured.

It is the purpose of this book to re-examine some of the basic principles on which the communicative approach is founded, to show why authentic texts should be at the centre of the foreign language learning process, and to propose ways in which teachers can broaden their scope for creative pedagogical initiatives.

We originally conceived the book as an aid for teachers using the *Authentik* newspapers and cassettes, which are now published in French, German, Spanish and English. The newspapers consist of (i) paste-ups of newspaper and magazine articles in the language in question, organized according to broad themes like "world news", "fashion", "sport", "holidays and travel", and (ii) a pedagogical section made up of information about the language learning process, exercises based on the corresponding cassette as well as the newspaper, a complete transcript of the cassette, and competitions for learners at various levels. The cassettes comprise recordings of radio news bulletins and other broadcasts, slow readings of some of these items, and interviews with native speakers; as far as possible their thematic content coincides with items in the corresponding newspaper. (For further information write to: Authentik Language Learning Resources Ltd, The O'Reilly Institute, Trinity College, Dublin 2.)

Although the book was planned in the first place with a specific audience in mind, its arguments and the pedagogical procedures we recommend are applicable to all authentic texts, wherever they come from and however they are presented to learners. The book is divided into four chapters, two of them theoretical in their orientation and two of them more practical. Chapter 1 briefly reviews some of the principal findings of language acquisition research and begins to consider what implications they have for language teaching. Chapter 2 goes on to examine the basic principles of communicative language teaching, with particular reference to the use of authentic texts. Chapter 3 then offers a practical working out of these principles in the form of a battery of exercise types for use with authentic texts, while Chapter 4 examines the role that authentic texts can play in developing learners' conscious control of the target language system. Finally, an appendix analyses the modern language exams set by Examination Boards in the United Kingdom.

An earlier version of the book was published in Ireland towards the end of 1988 under the title *Authentic Texts in Foreign Language Teaching: Theory and Practice*. In the earlier version Chapter 1 was written by Seán Devitt and David Singleton, Chapters 2 and 3 by David Little, and Chapter 4 by Seán Devitt, David Little acting as editor for the book as a whole. For this version, Chapter 1 has been revised by David Singleton, Chapters 2 and 3 have been revised by David Little, Chapter 4 has been revised by David Little and Seán Devitt, and Seán Devitt has written the appendix. David Little has again acted as editor.

As in the earlier version, we are glad to acknowledge our debt to the editors of the three editions of *Authentik* from which we have taken our examples and the groups of practising teachers who helped them month by month in the selection of materials and the devising of exercises: their efforts gave us a rich source to draw on. We are also glad to acknowledge our gratitude to the newspaper and magazine publishers who so generously allow us to reproduce their copyright material in *Authentik*.

David Little   Dublin
Seán Devitt   April 1989
David Singleton

Contents

Chapter 1

Language acquisition

Language
acquisition
research and
language
teaching

This chapter summarizes some of the principal findings of research into first and second language acquisition. The importance of such findings for the development of language teaching methodology cannot easily be exaggerated. After all, measures designed to assist the learning of foreign languages in a classroom environment are more likely to be successful if they take account of what we know about the mechanisms involved. Accordingly, the research findings reported here provide the essential theoretical underpinning for what follows in Chapters 2, 3 and 4.

"Acquisition"
and "learning"
.

The acquisition of a first language is almost by definition a natural process; and much of the research into second language acquisition has focussed on learning that has taken place outside a formal educational environment. However, research findings do not justify a hard and fast distinction between what is sometimes called "naturalistic" language acquisition on the one hand and the process of learning that goes on in a foreign language classroom on the other. Accordingly we use "acquisition" and "learning" interchangeably.

"Second" and
"foreign"
languages

It is sometimes useful to distinguish between "second" and "foreign" languages as between languages that respectively are and are not spoken in the community of which the learner is (at least temporarily) a member. However, in what follows "second language acquisition" should always be taken to refer to the learning of "foreign" as well as "second" languages.

1.1 The context of language acquisition

Over the last thirty years there has been a great deal of debate about the extent to which language acquisition is

Innate mechanisms that guide or determine language acquisition

guided or determined by innate mechanisms - variously referred to as "language acquisition device", "special programming", "bioprogram", etc. This is not the place to detail the evidence and arguments for and against the "innateness hypothesis". Language teachers are in the main interested in the question only to the extent that it affects the kinds of learning opportunities they need to provide - in other words, to the extent that an innate set of mechanisms may require a particular type of "feeding".

The central role of interaction in language acquisition

In fact, there is a fair degree of consensus concerning the kind of context that promotes language learning. Basically, the general view is that language learning is fostered by contexts which are rich in opportunities for interaction in and with the target language. "Interaction", as the formulation of the last sentence implies, has here a social and a psycholgogical sense.

Social interaction

Let us consider first the role of social interaction in language learning. It is perfectly clear that the normal way in which a child acquiring his or her first language gains experience in using that language is through exchanges to which the child and his or her caregiver(s) both make contributions of one kind or another. The following is a typical dialogue:

Child:	Mummy! Mummy!
Mother:	Yes, dear, what is it?
Child:	Soup.
Mother:	Oh yes, I see. You've upset your soup.

Structure of child-mother interaction parallels exchanges involving fully proficient speakers

What is interesting about this dialogue in terms of the manner in which the different contributions relate to each other is that it exactly parallels exchanges involving two fully proficient speakers. Thus we have the first speaker nominating the addressee ("Mummy!"), who in turn acknowledges contact and elicits the topic to be pursued. The first speaker then nominates the topic and the second speaker comments on it. One can very easily find adult-adult exchanges which precisely fit this structure, for example:

Nomination of addressee	**A:**	John.
Acknowledgement	**B:**	Yes.
Elicitation of topic		What is it?
Nomination of topic	**A:**	Look what I've done with the toothpaste.
Comment	**B:**	Oh Lord! What a mess!

It is not implausible to suppose, therefore, that exchanges like the child-mother dialogue above help accustom the child to the structure of face-to-face language use. Indeed, some researchers suggest that the child's initiation into the **The role of** rules of social interaction through language actually begins **pre-linguistic** before the emergence of speech in the child, with the "action **social** dialogue" characteristic of games such as giving and taking **interaction** routines, throwing and fetching routines, "peep-bo", etc.

To return to the specifically linguistic dimension, one notes that from the point at which children can contribute linguistically - however minimally - to dialogues with their caregivers, their contributions are constantly supported by **"Scaffolding"** what is sometimes called a "scaffolding" of adult input. This **provided by** allows the child space to contribute, while at the same time **fluent speaker** framing and expanding his or her contributions, often in such a way as to offer models of combinations that the child can only achieve through interaction with an adult or with a child who is already a fluent speaker. Thus:

Child:	Car
Father:	Yes, that's a car
Child:	Bu
Father:	Yes, it's a blue car

Indirect It is also the case, as the above example demonstrates, that **corrective** the adult's expansions provide a measure of indirect (and **feedback** thus non-threatening) corrective feedback with regard to **provided by** the formal aspects of the language being acquired.
fluent speaker

A further point about caregiver input that is worth noting is that such input seems (in most cultures, at least) to

Caregiver input
sensitive to the
child's interests
and capacities
be sensitive to the child's preoccupations, interests, experience, cognitive capacity and linguistic level. This does not mean that caregivers necessarily have very well-defined ideas about where the children they talk to are in developmental terms, nor that the adjustments they make to their speech are conscious and deliberate. What happens appears to be more in the nature of a subconscious or semiconscious response to various cues from the child indicating what are and are not going to be fruitful avenues to pursue in a given conversation, combined with a continuous monitoring (again, probably, largely subconscious) of how much of the input the child is understanding.

Native speakers
also provide
second language
learners with
"scaffolding"
and adjust input
to their needs
and capacities
Similar kinds of support are very frequently offered to second language learners by native speakers of the target language, language teachers, and even other learners. There is abundant evidence that the "scaffolding" described earlier in relation to first language development is also characteristic of much second language speech that is directed towards learners. Such speech often also tends to be adapted to the learner's specific needs and capacities, although the degree to which such "tuning" takes place appears to vary considerably according to the experience, personality and attitude of the speaker. We shall return to this question of fitting the input to the learner at a slightly later stage.

So far we have been looking at the question of social interaction in language learning in qualitative terms. However, we should not forget the very important dimension of quantity. There is obviously a fairly consistent correlation beween language learning outcomes and the amount of social interaction experienced in the target language. Children acquiring their first language spend an extremely high proportion of their waking hours engaged in such interaction. As far as second language learning is concerned, one need only point to the well-documented benefits of immersion programmes, or to the great difference it makes to language learning success if a learner can spend a few weeks or months living in the target language community.

4

First and
second
language
learning
possible
without social
interaction

Notwithstanding all of the foregoing, it is possible to overstate the importance of social interaction in language learning. There are language learners who make excellent progress despite having little or no opportunity to participate in social interaction through the language in question. For example, there are plenty of attested cases of children who have been so severely handicapped that they have been physically debarred from interacting with their caregivers through language but who have nevertheless acquired their caregivers' language - which, thanks to some technological advance, they have subsequently been able to use communicatively. Some such children have indeed gone on to become professional writers. Likewise, in the second language learning domain, there have always been stories in circulation about individuals who have managed to learn a second language from books alone (English from Shakespeare, Arabic from the Koran, etc.). Recent research in this area confirms that it is possible to learn a second language even if one's experience of that language is in a purely receptive mode.

Clearly, the only kind of interaction available to learners who have no access to social interaction in the target language is psychological interaction, by which we mean the psychological processing of target language input in such a way that it interlocks with and modifies the learner's existing knowledge. Of course, all learning depends on, one might

almost say is constituted by, psychological interaction in this sense; and in every language acquisition process a moment will sooner or later come when the learner is confronted with discourse which is not interactive in a social sense - a formal speech, a song, a newspaper article, a book, a film, a play, a television or radio programme, etc. - and which he or she will cope with and learn from without the benefit of social support.

There are strong indications from psychological and psycholinguistic research that the quality of a given psychological interaction relates to the extent to which the interactant sees the material being processed as having "personal singificance". This in turn, self-evidently, depends on the

Material that
learners find
significant is
more likely to
prompt "deep"
processing and
to be recalled
subsequently

relationship between the processed material and what the
interactant already knows, has already experienced, is currently preoccupied by, currently needs to know, etc. The
greater the personal significance factor, apparently, the
"deeper" the processing; and the "deeper" the processing,
the higher the chance of processed material being recalled
subsequently.

The implication of this evidence is that when, in the
context of social interaction, caregivers, native speakers,
teachers and peers "tune" their contributions to the interests and needs of their language learner interlocutors, they

not only render the interactions more meaningful, worth-
while, enjoyable etc. for their interlocutors, they also in-
crease the chances of some language being learned as a
result of these interactions. Indeed, the effectiveness of
social interaction in the target language as a promoter of
language learning may be largely due to the fact that, of its
nature, social interaction is bound to be at least to some
degree interlocutor-friendly.

The comment made above concerning quality and

quantity in respect of social interaction applies to all interaction with the target language. That is to say, if psychological interaction with samples of the target language needs to
be of a certain quality in order to promote efficient language
learning, it also needs to be plentiful.

To turn to the specific question of authentic texts as part
of a formal second language learning context, one of the
principal justifications for their use must be their capacity to

Authentic texts
have the
capacity to
enhance the
quality of
interaction in
and with the
target language

enhance the quality of interaction in and with the target
language. If carefully chosen so as to activate learners'
general world knowledge, to respond to and further stimu-
late learners' interests, and to address learners' preoccupations and worries, such texts can provide the basis for a
variety of social interactions in the target language. Precisely because they come complete with all the savour,
stench and rough edges of life beyond the school walls, they
are likely to be markedly more successful in provoking pupil
reaction and interaction than the somewhat anaemic texts
that one so often finds between the covers of textbooks. For

similar reasons, authentic texts, even when used in a non-social mode - as private reading matter or as a basis for individual language practice - are likely to give rise to a greater depth of psychological processing, and thus more learning, than specially written or simplified texts.

1.2 Developmental orders

The nature of first and second language development

Having considered the context in which language develops, let us now examine the nature of that development. We shall see that in some respects first language development and second language development appear to be remarkably similar, whereas in other respects they are quite different.

"Speech milestones" in first language acquisition

One phenomenon which characterizes first but not second language development is the series of age-related "speech milestones" which first language learners pass through in the early stages of their development. Whatever the first language being acquired and irrespective of the cultural milieu, a child will normally between one and two months of age begin to "coo" (that is, produce a range of vowel-like noises), between four and eight months start to "babble" (that is, produce combinations of a wide variety of consonant-like and vowel-like noises), between nine and eighteen months begin producing utterances composed of a single meaningful element, and between eighteen and twenty-four months start producing utterances in which two or three meaningful elements are combined under a single intonation contour.

No "speech milestones" in second language acquisition

"Milestones" of this kind do not feature in second language acquisition. It is usual for second language learners to begin producing utterances in their target language very soon after exposure to this language commences. Some researchers have, admittedly, argued that in situations where they are not immediately under pressure (e.g. from teachers) to produce target language output, second language learners tend to pass through a "silent period".

The "silent period" in second language acquisition

However, this silent period is customarily reckoned in weeks rather than months and years, and there is certainly no suggestion that second language learners revert in any circumstances to a cooing or babbling stage. Moreover, whenever second language learners do start producing target language utterances, these utterances are from the outset largely comprised of combinations of meaningful elements.

Similarities between first and second language acquisition as regards grammatical development

Resemblances between first and second language acquisition are, on the other hand, discernible in the grammatical aspects of language development - in the order in which grammatical affixes and linking elements (grammatical morphemes) emerge and in the evolution of function-differentiating ways of combining words into phrases and sentences (syntax).

When a first language acquirer begins to produce utterances constituted of more than one element, these elements are not in the initial stages signalled by the grammatical devices of adult language. Interestingly, the rate at which particular types of grammatical device are incorporated into the child's developing language system appears to be sensitive to the specific characteristics of the language being acquired. Thus, word-order stability seems to emerge earlier in English, where word order is relatively fixed and a fairly reliable indicator of sentential relations, than in the Romance languages, where word order is freer and more subject to variation related to focus, etc. Similarly, children acquiring as their mother tongue languages which depend heavily on changes in word-form for the signalling of grammatical relations and basic meaning categories, appear to acquire such morphology earlier than children acquiring more "syntactic" languages.

Rate of grammatical development sensitive to the specific characteristics of the language being acquired

However, although languages may differ from one another as regards the stage at which particular kinds of grammatical device appear, there is a not inconsiderable body of evidence that, as far as any individual language is concerned, the grammatical development of children acquiring that language as their mother tongue follows a broadly similar route. Thus, when grammatical affixes and linking devices begin to appear in the speech of children acquiring English as a first language, they seem to become established in a fairly stable order: the *-ing* ending (as in

Evidence that all learners of a particular first language follow a broadly similar route of grammatical development *going, playing, singing,* etc.) appears to be acquired relatively early, whereas the contracted copula *-'m, -'re, -'s* (as in *I'm, you're, she's,* etc.) appears to be acquired relatively late. Similarly, in their initial attempts to formulate *wh*-questions, acquirers of English as a first language consistently produce structures of the form *wh*-WORD + NOUN (PHRASE) + MAIN VERB (e.g. *What Dada cooking?*), go on to produce structures of the form *wh*-WORD + NOUN (PHRASE) + AUXILIARY + MAIN VERB (e.g. *What Dada is cooking?*), and only after these two phases have been traversed produce the adult language form *wh*-WORD + AUXILIARY + NOUN (PHRASE) + MAIN VERB (e.g. *What is Dada cooking?*).

To turn now to grammatical development in second language acquisition, the dominant view among researchers in this area is that for any given target language one can speak here too of a relatively predictable succession of developmental stages whose ordering is in broad terms unaffected either by the language background of learners or by the particularities of their learning situation. One must immediately add the qualification that this view is more widely accepted in respect of the evolution of syntactic structures than in respect of the order of acquisition of grammatical morphemes, owing to the fact that the methodology of many of the second language "morpheme studies" has been in some of its aspects questionable. Another point of distinction between second language grammatical morpheme research and second language syntax research is that the former has yielded findings which differ more from first language developmental orders than those yielded by the latter. For example, in the case of English, whereas there are numerous discrepancies between the average order of acquisition of the earliest learned grammatical morphemes discovered by first and second language acquisition research, with regard to the development of syntactic structures such as question and negative forms, such discrepancies are much less marked. Thus, while learners of English as a second language seem to pass through precisely the same phases in acquiring *wh*-questions as learners of English as a first language (see above), second language learners seem to acquire English possessive 's rather later than first language learners. On the other hand, even in relation to grammatical morpheme development one can, to the extent that one can trust the evidence, discern features in common between the second and the first language pattern. For example, English -*ing* seems to be acquired early irrespective of whether the language is being learned as a first or as a second language.

Can teachers really influence language learning?

A frequent reaction of language teachers when confronted with evidence of second language developmental orders is to pose the question: if the route of language learning is unaffected by the characteristics of the learning situation, why put effort into enlivening and enriching learners' classroom experience (by, for instance, introducing authentic materials)? The answer to this question comes essentially in four parts. The first concerns the reliability of the evidence; the second concerns those aspects of language learning which are left out of account in the claims about normal developmental orders; the third concerns the distinction between *route* and *rate* of development; and the fourth concerns the influence of consciously acquired and not yet automatized knowledge.

Doubts about the methodology of second language "morpheme studies"

Regarding the reliability of the evidence, mention has already been made of the doubts that have been raised about the methodology of many of the second language "morpheme studies". More generally, one should perhaps bear in mind the relative narrowness of the data-base on which current perspectives on second language acquisition are founded. This is certainly not to cast aspersions on the progress achieved by empirical approaches to second language acquisition research, nor to call into question the proposition that we now have vastly more information about second language acquisition than we had twenty years ago, when such approaches were getting under way. All that is being suggested here is that, in view of the fact that empirical second language acquisition research is still less than a quarter of a century old, one should beware of ascribing absolute definitiveness to present perceptions and models of the second language learning process.

Discussion of
second language
developmental
orders has said
little about
several central
aspects of
second language
development

On the question of what is left out of account in current discussion of second language developmental orders, one should note that such discussion has little or nothing to say about the development of the sound-system (phonological development), vocabulary (lexical development), or different context-related uses of the language (pragmatic development). First language acquisition research suggests that the sounds of a given language are mastered in a broadly predictable order by children acquiring it as mother tongue.

Phonological
development

The situation with regard to second language phonological development is less clear. As we noted above, little research has been conducted relative to this particular issue, and some of the research that has been done seems to indicate a kind of "translation" from first to second language phonology rather than a replication of the pattern observable in children acquiring the target language in question as a first language.

Lexical
development

As far as lexical development is concerned, again research in the second language area is scanty. In first language development, of course, early lexical development is vitally connected with basic concept development, and there is evidence in this context of a *phased* integration into the child's developing vocabulary system of certain kinds of relations between words and concepts. Whether this phenomenon also characterizes second language vocabulary development is not yet clear, but it is unlikely to be a major feature of second language learning which occurs beyond early childhood, given that older learners have already been through the process of acquiring and structuring basic concepts in their first language. In any case, no one has ever suggested (or is ever likely to!) that individual lexical items are acquired by second language learners in a fixed order.

Pragmatic
development

Similar kinds of points can be made about pragmatic development. Some researchers have argued that early first language development is driven by the child's communicative requirements and that these expand and diversify in step with early biological and social milestones, which are predictable. Later social development is, obviously, less predictable, and so, therefore, is the later course of diversification of language uses, whether in a first or a second language.

Factors that influence the rate of acquisition

As far as the *route-rate* distinction is concerned, both first and second language research and experience suggest that, while differing amounts and types of input may not influence the general *route* of grammatical development (but cf. below), such factors do have a significant impact on *rate* of development. Speech therapists commonly report, for example, that parents who imagine that their children need special treatment for retarded speech development can often be led to effect the "cure" themselves by being encouraged simply to talk to their children more. In the second language domain, research indicates that a combination of meaningful social interaction in the target language and instruction promotes more rapid language learning progress than either social interaction or instruction alone.

Consciously learned, non-automatized knowledge can help learners to perform beyond their general developmental stage in some circumstances

This reference to instruction brings us to the fourth part of our answer to the question about the relationship between language learning experience and language learning progress, which has to do with the influence of consciously acquired and not yet automatized knowledge. Up to this point our discussion has proceeded on the basis of the premise that grammatical developmental orders are not affected by variables in the learning situation. However, this premise is actually something of a simplification, since it does not take into account the effect of learners giving conscious attention to rules and paradigms. This effect seems to be limited. The indications are that it does not interfere with the manifestation of the normal developmental orders in casual, informal, fluent speech but that it may result in the masking of normal developmental orders in circumstances which require a high degree of attention to formal accuracy and allow time for formal fine-tuning. In other words, by drawing on consciously learned, non-automatized material, second language learners can on occasion perform at a level beyond their general developmental stage - which in some situations can clearly be very useful.

By way of conclusion to this section, let us explore some

of the practical implications of the ground it has covered. One of these has to do with attitudes towards error. There has been a fair amount of talk in recent years about "error tolerance". This expression is unfortunate insofar as it can be misinterpreted as a socio-political position - as "going soft" on error. That is actually the very opposite of what is required. Recent research certainly suggests that deviations are an inevitable part of language development and that it makes no sense - actually in terms of hard realism - to treat all error as evidence of laziness, negligence or ineptitude. However, recent research also indicates that we do not have to be "tolerant" of error in the sense of resigning ourselves to the same errors appearing in learners' output *ad infinitum*. On the contrary, it appears to show that we can take steps to accelerate learners' progress through each error-making stage and to give them the tools to outperform in some circumstances their general developmental level. These steps consist, essentially, in the provision of a language learning environment which is rich in target language input of an appropriate kind, and which caters for some measure of consciousness-raising in relation to aspects of the target language system. Authentic materials, exploited in the ways outlined in Chapters 3 and 4, can make a unique contribution to the creation of such an environment.

Attitudes towards error

Error an inevitable part of language development

Helping learners to overcome error

The role of authentic materials

1.3 The influence of the mother tongue

We have already mentioned some differences between first and second language acquisition. However, we have not yet referred to the most obvious difference of all. Whereas the beginning first language learner (unless he or she is learning two parental languages simultaneously) has experience of just one language, the second language learner, by definition, has encountered at least two. Moreover, in many countries typical second language learners first encounter their second language during the course of formal education, which means that they have a well-developed mastery of their first language before coming into contact with their second. From what we know about human

The most obvious difference between first and second language learners

learning generally, it would be extraordinary if such learners' dealings with their new language were entirely uninfluenced by what they have already experienced of and in their mother tongue.

Influence of first language on second language development and performance

In fact, as any language teacher knows, the influence of a second language learner's first language on his or her progress and performance in the second is usually fairly readily apparent. Traditionally, this influence has been perceived in largely negative terms. References to it in language teaching manuals produced in the first half of this century and earlier tend to consist in warnings about the dangers of lapsing into "Anglicisms", in "rogues galleries" of "false friends" (i.e. deceptive cognates), etc.

Audio-lingual methodology saw second language learning as habit formation

This general attitude persisted through the period when "audio-lingual" methodology was dominant - that is, from the late 1950s to the early 1970s. The psychological assumptions on which audio-lingual courses (and the audio-visual courses which developed out of them) were based were essentially behaviourist in nature; chief among them was the assumption that language acquisition was a matter of "conditioning", of appropriate responses to stimuli being "reinforced" in one way or another until they became automatized as "habits". On this view, learning a second language consisted in the formation of a second set of habits,

Positive and negative transfer and interference

a process which would be "facilitated" by "positive transfer" where the new habits to be learned coincided with already established first language habits, but "inhibited" or "interfered with" by "negative transfer" where there were divergences between first language habits and target patterns. In principle, therefore, the behaviourist account recognized both the negative and the positive aspect of cross-linguistic influence. However, because the principal preoccupation in language teaching circles was, not unnaturally, the eradication of error, in practice greater emphasis was placed on the "interference" problem. The response to this problem

The attempt to predict "inteference" errors by "contrastive analysis"

proposed at the time was to attempt to predict interference errors by means of a "contrastive analysis" of the native and target systems and to forestall such errors by intensively drilling those parts of the target language which showed marked differences from the learners' first language.

The success of contrastive analysis was somewhat mixed. One major problem with it was its failure to recognize the fact that many aspects of second language development seem closely to resemble aspects of first language development and are not directly or uniquely relatable to cross-linguistic influence; errors of a "developmental" kind were thus simply not predicted by contrastive analysis. Another was its association with the behaviourist account of language learning, which was increasingly under attack. In sum, there was widespread disillusionment with contrastive analysis in the 1970s - a disillusionment which in some circles led to claims that the cross-linguistic dimension of second language learning was of little or no significance.

Shortcomings of contrastive analysis

A clearly more sensible response was that of those researchers who sought to decouple the notion of cross-linguistic influence from the behaviourist view of language learning and to explore ways in which it could be integrated into accounts of second language learning which gave full weight to the active, creative role of the learner's internal processing mechanisms and communication strategies. In fact, far from being incompatible with a view of language acquisition which lays stress on developmental processes, cross-linguistic influence can now be seen as intimately bound up with such processes. Thus, for example, the presence of a particular structure in a learner's mother tongue may accelerate or retard that learner's progress through the series of developmental phases associated with the acquisition of the corresponding target structure, depending on whether the native language structure resembles a version of the target structure characteristic of an intermediate developmental stage in its acquisition of the final, native-like version.

New approaches to cross-linguistic influence

Another very interesting aspect of recent research into cross-linguistic influence has been the exploration of the relationship between such influence and "communication strategies" used by second language learners to circumvent difficulties when actually performing in their target language. For instance, it has been shown that where a particu-

Cross-linguistic influence and "communication strategies"

15

lar target language structure is very different from the corresponding structure in the first language, learners will often avoid the difficulty simply by shaping their target language utterances in such a way that they are not obliged to use the structure in question.

Covering a
lexical gap by
"borrowing"

A further example of a cross-linguistically related communication strategy is the phenomenon of "borrowing", whereby a learner covers a lexical gap in his or her target language knowledge by using an item derived from his or her first language - which may be "converted" so as to sound or look like a target language item. The degree to which such borrowing takes place is apparently sensitive to the learner's

"Borrowing"
from second as
well as first
languages

perception of the degree of relatedness between the two languages in question. In fact, not only first language knowledge but also knowledge of other second languages may be brought into play for borrowing purposes, depending on the relevant perceived typological distances involved. So, for example, a German-speaking learner of Spanish who also has a knowledge of French will quickly come to realize that, in the context of an interaction through Spanish, items borrowed from French are more likely to succeed communicatively than items borrowed from German, and will act accordingly.

Sensitizing
learners to
similarities and
differences
between their
first and second
languages

Finally in this connection, it may be worth mentioning some experiments that have been conducted in the sharpening of second language learners' awareness of similarities and differences between their first and second languages. This sensitization has been effected by means of an array of classroom activities of an explicitly comparative/contrastive kind. The results of such experiments suggest that raising linguistic consciousness in this cross-linguistic manner can be helpful in dealing with second language difficulties which may be otherwise intractable.

A more positive
role for the
cross-linguistic
factor in second
language
learning

The effect of such findings is to allow the cross-linguistic factor in second language learning and performance to be seen in a rather more positive light - in terms not of inadequate conditioning, but rather of strategic avoidance and gap-filling, of linguistic sensitivity and of a normal, perhaps inevitable, dimension to the second language developmental process. There have always been linguists who have claimed that it is actually *through* our first language knowledge that we gain entry into a second language. Whether or not this proposition is literally true, it is now indisputable that there are circumstances and respects in which the role of the first language in second language acquisition and use is anything but negative. One very good example of the positive role of cross-linguistic influence, and one which is highly relevant in the present context, is the way in which the general meaning of an authentic foreign language text can often be understood by people with little or no knowledge of the language in question, simply on the basis of cognate recognition.

The positive role of cross-linguistic influence in coping with authentic texts

1.4 Attitude and motivation in second language learning

The role of attitude: a major difference between first and second language learning

Another major difference between the child in the early stages of acquiring his or her mother tongue and the child or adolescent learning a second language at school is that the latter is at a stage of cognitive develoment that enables him or her to form an attitude towards the learning task in question, whereas this can hardly be said of the former. Indeed, the baby acquiring his or her first language is not even aware of a learning task. Very young children acquiring a second language "naturalistically" may also have a rather limited awareness of a language learning process as opposed to or distinct from their efforts to engage in communication through the second language. However, children learning a second language at school - whether or not under a "communicative" regime - perceive that language from the outset as having roughly the same status as other subjects on the timetable. This means that they see it as likely to make roughly the same demands on their retentive capacity, and they fairly quickly begin to evaluate the second language learning experience and to rate it relative to other areas of the curriculum.

Children learning a second language at school inevitably develop attitudes to the learning task

It is a commonplace among teachers that a pupil's attitude and motivation in respect of a given subject are crucial. There is undoubtedly a great deal of truth in this proposition; the trouble is, though, that attitude and motivation are extremely nebulous and elastic concepts and it is thus difficult to demonstrate how *precisely* they relate to learning success. With particular regard to second language learning, research undertaken over the last twenty years or so suggests that, whatever else one may say about the nature of this relationship, it is neither uniform for all circumstances nor unidirectional.

"Attitude" and "motivation" difficult concepts to pin down

Language teachers often observe that learners who do well tend to be those who are interested in or favourably disposed towards the culture associated with their target language and the people who speak it. On the other hand, there is plenty of evidence, from both research and everyday experience, that immigrants who feel, or are made to feel, alienated from the life of the community in which they find themselves (Hispanics in the United States, Turks in West Germany, etc.) often fail to acquire more than the most rudimentary command of the language of that community. The obvious inference is that the degree of social and psychological distance that exists between a learner and the target language community is of critical importance in relation to the degree of proficiency which that learner will achieve in the language in question.

Social and psychological distance as factors in second language acquisition

However, other research suggests that life is not quite this simple. One very well known line of investigation in this area begins by drawing a basic distinction between an *integrative* orientation towards the target language community and culture, that is, a positive desire to interact with that community and culture, and an *instrumental* orientation, in other words a utilitarian perspective which sees knowledge of the target language as a means to an end such as further education, employment or a higher salary. Many learners show some measure of both orientations, but mostly one or the other seems to predominate. What is interesting in the present connection, though, is that the effect of the dominance of one or the other orientation seems to vary from learning situation to learning situation. Where learners find it relatively easy to make contact with the target language

"Integrative" & "instrumental" orientations in second language learning

Correlation of these orientations with successful learning seems to vary from one learning situation to another community (e.g. learners of French in certain parts of Canada) it appears to be the integrative orientation which is correlated with greater learning success. Where, on the other hand, the target language is being learned essentially as an international *lingua franca* far from any major population centre of the target language community (e.g. English in the Philippines), success seems to be correlated with instrumental orientation.

Relation between positive motivation and successful learning

To complicate matters further, it is not always entirely clear what the causal relationship is in correlations between attitude/motivation and second language learning success. Some research findings seem to indicate that favourable attitudes towards the target language community actually *develop out of* rather than *underlie* success in learning the second language. If this is so, then clearly language learning success must itself be taken into account as a factor in determining quality of learner motivation. Hence the prevalence of versions of the diagram below in treatments of the role of motivation in second language learning.

Motivation that arises from the learning situation

If one takes a broad view of language learning success and interprets as success any positive experience which is connected with or results from language learning, one can link the above model to what some commentators have referred to as *internal* sources of motivation, that is, sources of motivation which arise out of the language learning situation as opposed to those which are brought to that situation by the learner. Obvious examples are the general atmosphere in which learning takes place, the degree of relevance of the syllabus, and the interest presented by learning materials and activities.

Positive attitude and motivation go hand in hand with successful second language learning

To summarize, research tends to confirm the widespread intuition that a favourable attitude and a high level of motivation go hand in hand with second language learning success. However, different kinds of motivation seem to be optimal in different situations, and the nature of the learning experience may itself be a powerful influence in determining attitude and motivation. Authentic texts can fairly obviously have a role in fostering contact with and interest in the culture of the target language and, if sensitively chosen, in making the learning experience enjoyable. With regard to the more "instrumental" dimension, certain kinds of authentic text can be extremely effective in raising learners' consciousness about the career and leisure opportunities that a competence in the language in question makes available.

Authentic texts and motivation

Suggestions for further reading

A good general introduction to first language acquisition is Alison J. Elliot's *Child Language* (Cambridge University Press; 1981). Roger Brown's *A First Language* (Cambridge, Mass.: Harvard University Press; 1973) is highly readable but is confined to the acquisition of English.

Two excellent introductions to second language acquisition research are W. T. Littlewood's *Foreign and Second Language Learning* (Cambridge University Press; 1984) and Rod Ellis's *Understanding Second Language Acquisition* (Oxford University Press; 1985). The former is quite short and very much oriented towards language teaching issues, whereas the latter gives a fuller account and has a somewhat more theoretical orientation. *Language Two*, by H. Dulay, M. Burt and S. Krashen (New York & London: Oxford University Press; 1982) draws pedagogical conclusions from research findings, especially in those areas with which its authors are particularly associated. *Second Language Acquisition: a Book of Readings*, edited by E. Hatch (Rowley, Mass.: Newbury House; 1978) is a collection of detailed research reports, most of them dealing with the acquisiton of English. H. Wode's *Learning a Second Language 1. An Integrated View of Language Acquisition* (Tübingen: Gunter Narr; 1981) combines an excellent discussion of theoretical issues with a fascinating account of his own children's acquisition of English.

D. Singleton's article "The fall and rise of language transfer" (in *The Advanced Language Learner*, ed. J. A. Coleman & R. Towell; London: CILT; 1988) surveys the successive phases of research into the influence of the mother tongue on second language learning. For a more complete review of relevant research see H. Ringbom's *The Role of the First Language in Foreign Language Learning* (Clevedon: Multilingual Matters; 1987).

A very useful introduction to the role of attitude and motivation in second language learning is provided by the chapter on motivation in S. McDonough's *Psychology in Foreign Language Teaching* (London: Allen & Unwin; 1981). For a more detailed account see R. Gardner's *Social Psychology and Second Language Learning: the Role of Attitudes and Motivation* (London: Arnold; 1985).

Chapter 2

The communicative approach and authentic texts

Purpose of this chapter
The purpose of this chapter is to summarize the principles that underpin the communicative approach in general and the use of authentic texts as a main source of target language input in particular. Although the communicative approach did not arise directly from language acquisition research, we shall see that in its fundamentals it coincides closely with the findings of that research. We shall also see that the increasingly central role that authentic texts have come to occupy in communicative language teaching methodology can be justified as much in terms of language acquisition research findings as in terms of basic communicative principles.

The communicative approach and second language acquisition research

2.1 Communicative principles

Determining features of the communicative approach
The communicative approach to language teaching derives its name and its essential character from the fact that at every stage - the setting of learning targets, the definition of a syllabus, the development of learning materials, the elaboration and implementation of classroom activities, and the assessment of learners' progress - it focuses on language as a medium of communication. In this it differs from the traditions in language teaching that it seeks to replace. Both the grammar-translation and the audio-lingual/audio-visual methods focus from first to last on the grammatical system of the target language (no doubt both methods would claim to be teaching languages for communication, but that is a different matter). The communicative methodologies that have emerged over the past decade and a half have insisted with increasing confidence on the importance of engaging learners in activities which require them

Fundamental difference between the communicative approach and the traditions it seeks to replace to communicate in the target language. We saw in Chapter 1 that children learn their mother tongue *as* they communicate. By promoting learning not just *for* but *through* communication the communicative approach aligns itself with one of the basic facts of "naturalistic" language acquisition.

In its most rigorous form, perhaps best exemplified by the "threshold level" specifications and related documents produced by the Council of Europe's modern languages projects, the communicative approach never loses sight of the fact that all communication takes place in a physical setting and between participants, and has a social purpose. The typical communicative syllabus begins by considering who its learners are in terms of such characteristics as age, educational background, and previous language learning experience. It then goes on to define the needs that the learners will satisfy by learning the target language, including the communicative purposes that competence in the language will enable them to fulfil. This makes it possible to describe in some detail the kinds of language behaviour that successful learners should be capable of at the end of their course of learning. Thus the learner-centredness of the communicative approach arises directly from an analysis of the social functions of language.

Probably the two most widespread misconceptions about the communicative approach are (i) that it is concerned exclusively with the spoken language, and (ii) that it is indifferent to grammar. The first misconception probably arose because the earliest communicative projects were concerned with learners whose principal need was for a basic competence in oral communication. The Council of Europe's "threshold level" specifications were originally designed to fulfil the needs of migrant workers; and the Graded Objectives movement in the United Kingdom was conceived as a way of bringing foreign language learning within the realistic reach of pupils of lower ability. But it is obvious that in literate societies written language performs a multitude of communicative purposes, so that reading and writing can be as important as listening and speaking in some communicative curricula. (At the same time, because

Emphasis on communication as a social activity results in learner-centredness

Two common misconceptions about the communicative approach

Communicative approach not concerned exclusively with spoken language

the methods of western education depend so thoroughly on literacy skills, it is easy for teachers to overlook the fact that the great majority of people, including some of the most highly educated, make relatively little use of the writing skill in their daily life once full-time education is behind them.)

Communicative approach not indifferent to grammar

The belief that the communicative approach is indifferent to grammar seems to take two forms. On the one hand there are those who believe that it is hostile to the explicit treatment of grammar as a matter of pedagogical principle. This is not so; indeed, the earliest communicative documents emphasized the need for an eclectic methodology rather than one conforming to any particular orthodoxy. On the other hand there are those who maintain that because the communicative approach is above all interested in exchanges of meaning, it fails to give grammatical form its

The relation between form and meaning

due. There are two answers to this argument. First, in all languages form and meaning are closely interrelated. It is true that we often succeed in communicating our intended meanings despite formal inadequacies of one kind or another - this frequently happens to all of us not only in foreign languages but also in our first language. However, there is a point beyond which disregard of grammatical form virtually guarantees a breakdown in communication. In a very real sense communication depends on grammar. Secondly, although much communicative methodology gives meaning priority over form, this merely emphasizes the importance of exploring formal issues within a meaningful context; it does not amount to a disregard of grammar. On the

The importance of exploring formal issues within a context of meaning

contrary, because meaning and form are closely interrelated, a central part of the communicative purpose is to discover means of enabling learners to understand more acutely how the forms of their target language are organized in the creation of meaning. How we can use authentic texts to achieve this is the principle concern of Chapter 4.

2.2 Authentic texts and the communicative approach

From the beginning "authenticity" has been one of the key concepts of the communicative movement in language teaching. After all, if we are primarily concerned with language as a medium of communication, we shall want to ensure that there is a strong thread of continuity between what goes on in our classrooms and the characteristic modes of communication in our target language community. A major problem with language teaching methodologies that are centred on the target language system is precisely that they all too easily leave the learner without secure bridges into the actual world of language use. If its claims are to have any validity, the communicative approach must foster actual communication through the target language in the classroom; for only then can we be sure that our learners are able to communicate through the language. Again we are forcibly reminded of the fact that "naturalistic" language acquisition occurs *through* communication.

The need to build bridges into the real world of communication

Any course of learning involves four obligatory factors: a learner, a goal, content, and a process. The communicative approach is concerned to observe the principle of authenticity in regard to each of them. In other words, it is concerned that in every dimension the course of learning should be appropriate to the learner's needs, expectations and experience on the one hand and to the realities of communication in the target language community on the other.

The communicative approach and authenticity in four dimensions: learner, goal, content and process

Essentially an authentic text is a text that was created to fulfil some social purpose in the language community in which it was produced. Thus novels, poems, newspaper and magazine articles, handbooks and manuals, recipes, and telephone directories are all examples of authentic texts; and so too are radio and television broadcasts and computer programmes. As far as language teaching is concerned, however, "authentic text" has come to have a rather more limited meaning than this. Many attempts to implement the communicative approach have found no use for literary texts (sometimes this is entirely appropriate to the learners' needs, but often it reflects a prejudice against the study of literary texts as a hangover from the grammar-translation method); and even in the last quarter of the twentieth century the physical reality of most classrooms prohibits the

"Authentic text" defined

In language teaching "authentic text" often given a rather narrow meaning frequent use of video or computer materials. Accordingly, when language teachers use the term "authentic text" they often mean a piece of writing that originally appeared in a newspaper or magazine and is probably of ephemeral value and interest. Most language course books published in the past decade have contained their share of authentic texts in this sense of the term. The problem is, of course, that such texts are usually out of date before the course book is published - which was the chief reason for introducing the Authentik newspapers and cassettes in the first place.

There are essentially three reasons why well-chosen authentic texts should occupy a central role in any second language learning process. First, because they have been written for a communicative purpose they are more interesting than texts which have been invented to illustrate the usage of some feature of the target language; learners are thus likely to find them more motivating than invented texts. Secondly, because they revolve around content rather than form, authentic texts are more likely to have acquisition-promoting content than invented texts. This is partly because they provide a richer linguistic diet, and partly because they encourage learners to concentrate on penetrating to the meaning that lies beneath the surface structures. Thirdly, if used in sufficient quantities authentic texts can begin to replicate the "language bath" in which the first language learner is immersed from birth. Clearly, the child learning its first language or the adult immersed in a second language community enjoys an infinitely higher level of exposure to the target language than can easily be provided by a language classroom at some distance from the target language community. Of course, the teacher can begin to replicate the conditions of "naturalistic" acquisition by using the target language as the normal medium of classroom management and instruction. But a large and varied diet of authentic texts is essential if she is to create a genuinely acquisition-rich environment. In the foreign language classroom authentic texts can serve as a partial substitute for the community of native speakers within which "naturalistic" language acquisition occurs; the more authentic texts we confront our learners with, the more opportunities we shall create for acquisition to take place. Once again the findings of language acquisition research support commonsense intuitions.

"Vertical" and "horizontal" structures: authentic texts as facilitators of natural acquisition processes

We noted in Chapter 1 that children typically acquire the forms of their mother tongue *after* they have learned how to participate in highly organized interaction. We might expand the point by saying that they first master the "vertical" structures of discourse, and that this provides them with the framework within which they master the "horizontal" structures of syntax and morphology. Thus they acquire language in the very process of using it as a more or less efficient medium of communication: mastery of "horizontal" structures arises from constant practice in the communication of meaning within "vertical" structures. The use of authentic texts as the chief source of target language input allows the second language learner to follow a similar course of development.

Three kinds of knowledge required for comprehension

Comprehension is an essential component of communication, and thus a precondition for efficient language acquisition. It requires access to three kinds of knowledge. First,

Knowledge of the world

we need to be able to draw on knowledge of the world, the ever increasing stock of facts and hypotheses that we accumulate from the business of attentive living. This enables us to fix our general bearings and provides us with what might be described as a "plausibility filter": the meanings that we attach to utterances and texts do not conflict with our world

Discourse knowledge

knowledge. Secondly, we need to be able to draw on knowledge of the norms of discourse. This knowledge tells us what kind of communicative event we are involved in and helps us to generate appropriate expectations of its structure and outcome. Thirdly, we need to be able to draw on

Linguistic knowledge

our gradually developing linguistic knowledge, that is, our knowledge of the grammar of the language in question.

Comprehension and authentic texts

It is often assumed that authentic texts are more difficult for language learners to cope with than invented texts. If coping is a matter of word-for-word translation, this may well be the case. But the comprehension on which effective language acquisition depends is not a matter of word-for-word translation - the child learning its first language cannot, after all, use translation as an aid to learning. It is our contention that if they are properly handled, authentic texts promote acquisition because they challenge learners to activate relevant knowledge of the world, of discourse, and of the language system, and thus construct the conditions for further learning. The essential point is that authentic texts appropriate to a particular group of learners will belong to text types and deal with topics with which those learners are already more or less familiar. Clearly, they will need to be provided with various aids to comprehension, but they themselves will be able to contribute much in the way of understanding by drawing on their existing knowledge.

What we have said so far about authentic texts in relation to language acquisition processes reaffirms the communicative principle that meaning has priority over form. The argument of the preceding paragraphs assumes that authentic texts should be used authentically: that their exploitation in the classroom should be shaped by a general awareness that they were written for a particular communicative purpose. At the same time, however, we must not overlook the fact that native speakers sometimes focus on form, using their knowledge of the grammar of their mother tongue in order to understand structurally complex passages, or reading authentic texts with a view to enhancing their competence in their mother tongue. In the same way authentic texts provide a living context for the treatment of grammar for foreign language learners.

2.3 From reception to production

Reduced to its most basic terms, our argument is that authentic texts should constitute the primary source of input in any course of language learning because in the classroom only authentic texts can create a sufficiently acquisition-rich environment. Our concern in the remainder of this book is with the question: how do we help our learners to turn *input* into *intake*? In most examinations and many course books, authentic texts are used principally as the basis for compre-

How authentic texts promote language acquisition

The priority of meaning over form

Using authentic texts authentically

Authentic texts and the treatment of grammar

Our argument reduced to basic terms

Converting "input" into "intake"

hension exercises; but if there is any substance in the claims we have made above, work on authentic texts must be capable of going beyond reception to production.

Traditional approaches to the teaching of productive skills

Traditional approaches to the teaching of productive skills in a foreign language start with the forms of words, then move on to syntax at sentence level, and finally combine sentences in discourse. This building-blocks approach makes an undeniable appeal to common sense. However,

A different approach implied by our model of language acquisition

the model of language acquisition that we presented in Chapter 1 and have appealed to throughout this chapter moves in the opposite direction: world and discourse knowledge are used to establish a broad framework of comprehension within which linguistic knowledge is then developed. In Chapters 3 and 4 we shall recommend a pedagogical approach based on this model

Words and their role in the productive process

For the sake of clarity it is necessary to say something here about words. By suggesting that activities designed to promote productive skills should take discourse as their starting point, we do not mean to imply that words somehow come last in the productive process. On the contrary, at all

The importance of words at all levels

levels of linguistic reflection and analysis nothing can be achieved without words. We recall much of our world knowledge and refer to all of it in words; and the structure of any discourse depends crucially on the words we use. It is not words themselves that should be our final concern in the productive process, however, but the way in which they combine with one another. We also do not mean to imply

The productive process not straightforward

that the productive process is a straightforward matter of moving downwards through a hierarchy of functions. Constructing an appropriate piece of discourse involves planning, production and monitoring on various levels, and we move up and down through these levels with great flexibility.

A look ahead to Chapter 3

In Chapter 3 we examine some of the activities and exercise types that have been used with authentic texts and begin to suggest how the model of language learning we have presented in this and the previous chapter can be implemented. In particular we seek to show how learners

Exploiting what learners already know

can exploit the knowledge that they bring to the learning task. We assume that they are capable of much more

Giving learners
time and space
in which to
learn
creative work than is often supposed, always provided they are given time and space in which to learn. In this connection it should be noted that the activities and exercise types we recommend are capable of fostering a high degree of learner autonomy. We attach great importance to this, for

logically only those who achieve a significant level of autonomy as language learners are likely to have the confidence to remain adventurous and efficient language users throughout their adult life.

Suggestions for further reading

The most important of the Council of Europe's communicative language syllabuses are *The Threshold Level* by J. van Ek (Strasbourg; 1975), *Un Niveau Seuil* by D. Coste, J. Courtillon, V. Ferenczi, M. Martins-Baltar & E. Papo (Strasbourg; 1976), and *Kontaktschwelle* by M. Baldegger, M. Müller, G. Schneider & A. Näf (Strasbourg; 1980). *Languages Step by Step: Graded Objectives in the UK*, by B. Page & S. Rowell (London: CILT; 1987) provides a useful overview of attempts to implement a communicative approach in British schools. For an up-to-date account of the evolution of communicative syllabus design see D. Nunan's *Syllabus Design* (Oxford University Press; 1988).

H. G. Widdowson's *Teaching Language as Communication* (Oxford University Press; 1978) is one of the most durable contributions to the debate on communicative language teaching. Its concern with language as discourse means that it contains a wealth of material relevant to the use of authentic texts in second language teaching. The same concern characterizes most of the articles and papers in Widdowson's two collections, *Explorations in Applied Linguistics I* and *Explorations in Applied Linguistics II* (Oxford University Press; 1979 & 1984).

Interactive Language Teaching, edited by W. M. Rivers (Cambridge University Press; 1987), reflects the growing concern of methodologists to provide for as much interaction as possible, not only between learners as they use their target language to communicate with one another but also between the individual learner and the target language.

Chapter 3

Exercise types for use with authentic texts

Purpose of
this chapter
This chapter discusses and illustrates some of the exercises and activities that can be used to bring learners into sustained interaction with authentic texts. Our textual examples and many of the exercises attached to them are taken from issues of *Authentik* published in 1987-8. It should be noted, however, that because many of our examples originally formed part of exercise chains, their original purpose may have been somewhat different from the one described in our analysis. By including examples in three Examples in
three languages languages we hope to give readers the opportunity to work through some exercises without the benefit of fluency, as though they were learners themselves. Although our discussion is confined to printed texts, many of the activities we shall mention can also be used, with or without adaptation, with audio texts.

Structure
and content
of this chapter
We begin the chapter by summarizing our general principles, which follow directly from Chapters 1 and 2; then we look at the forms of comprehension exercise that have traditionally been used with authentic texts and consider their limitations as well as their usefulness; we go on to outline an approach to comprehension that is based on productive activities designed to overcome these limitations; and we conclude the chapter by considering how to use authentic texts as a basis for productive exercises.

3.1 General principles
General aims of
communicative
language
teaching
Communicative language teaching that assigns a central role to authentic texts should be characterized by three general aims. First, in common with other versions of the communicative approach, it should aim to give learners a

communicative competence in the target language corresponding to their needs, expectations and interests. This aim reminds us (as we saw in Chapter 2) that communication is a social activity, but also that the learner is an individual. Secondly, our approach should aim to help learners to develop, as part of their communicative competence, the capacity to make an authentic response to authentic texts; that is, a response to texts as communicative events and not just examples of the target language. Thirdly, since authentic texts will in principle be available to learners long after they have left school, our approach should aim to encourage them to learn for life. In other words, we should want them to become confident that at any time in the future they can pick up a newspaper or magazine in their target language, understand it, react to it, and learn from it. This means that work on authentic texts should be explicitly concerned to develop learners' autonomy.

In deciding how best to fulfil these aims we need a model of the language learning process. In Chapter 1 we saw how all "naturalistic" language acquisition takes place *through* interaction and *through* communication, and in Chapter 2 we argued that communicative language teaching is essentially defined in these terms. In Chapter 2 we also argued that a large part of the rationale for using authentic texts as a central component of language teaching resides in the capacity of such texts to create an acquisition-rich environment in which learners can interact not only with one another but also with the target language. It is important to stress this latter form of interaction. Most methodological proposals for communicative language teaching assign a central role to group and pair work as a means of creating the conditions for communication in the classroom. This reflects the fact that all linguistic communication is in some sense social activity, and it provides for the possibility of learning *through* communication. However, we must not overlook the fact that social interaction is not all that is involved in successful language learning. All learners, whether they are children learning their first language or adolescents or adults learning a second language, need time

Communicative competence and learners' needs·

An authentic response to authentic texts

Learning for life

A model of the language learning process

Group and pair work in the communicative approach

Learning as an individual process

and space in which to integrate the new material that they learn with what they already know. No doubt the process of integration can begin during social interaction, but its successful completion requires that learners spend time on their own (sometimes when they are in the presence of others).

Methodological implications of our model of language learning:

This model of the language learning process implies the following general methodological principles:

... target language as medium of instruction ...

(i) As far as possible the target language should be the language of classroom management and instruction. This may seem a hopeless aspiration to those who habitually teach foreign languages through English; but the fact is that teaching through the medium of the target language requires a relatively limited repertoire on the part of the teacher and a very limited repertoire on the part of the learner. This principle should also extend to written instructions for exercises and activities, though it is not always complied with in the examples that follow.

... learning by communicating through the target language ...

(ii) Many of the exercises and activities used should require learners to communicate with one another through the target language, which implies a large measure of group and pair work.

... some essential parts of the learning process are solitary

(iii) Some exercises and activities should be designed explicitly to help learners integrate new material with what they already know. This implies a recognition that essential parts of the learning process are solitary (some of them of course work below the level of consciousness). It is important to remember that learners can be on their own while remaining in the physical presence of thirty other learners.

3.2 Focus on comprehension

(i) Traditional approaches

Comprehension questions

Our first four examples are of traditional types of comprehension exercise, using multiple-choice or open questions in English or the target language. These are also the means used to test comprehension of written texts in public examinations. It is worth working through these four examples carefully (however little Spanish or German one may know), trying to capture the techniques one uses in arriving at an answer.

EXAMPLE 1

Encuentran lleno de cerdos un turismo robado en Orense
Orense, **Efe**

Un turismo Seat 850, que le había sido sustraído al vecino de San Ciprián de Viñas E.B.M., fue recuperado horas después por la Policía en la avenida de Zamora, cargado con cerdos de tres y cuatro meses.

Según la denuncia formulada en Comisaría, el propietario había dejado estacionado su vehículo en las immediaciones de su domicilio, de donde desapareció en el curso de la mañana del martes.

Efectivos policiales localizaron el vehículo horas después, en la capital de la provincia y con media docena de cerdos que ocupaban la parte posterior del turismo, alguno de ellos sobre los propios asientos.

El turismo tenía hecho el puente en el sistema de encendido y, por estar bastante deteriorado, su propietario no lo había valorado en más de cinco mil pesetas. Una vez recuperado, el ganado fue trasladado por la Policía al recinto en el que se celebra la feria de ganado.

(*ABC Jueves*, 31.12.87)

Open questions in English

Choose the correct answers from the following:
1. (a) the car was stolen with 3 or 4 pigs in it
   (b) the car was empty when stolen
   (c) there were some pigs in the car when it was stolen
2. (a) the owner parked the car near his home
   (b) he left the car near the police station
   (c) the car was stolen immediately after it was parked
3. (a) half a dozen policemen found the car
   (b) a tourist was also in the back of the car
   (c) there were pigs in the back of the car
4. (a) the car was worth much more than 5,000 pesetas
   (b) the car was started without a key (hot-wired)
   (c) a party was held to celebrate the recovery of the pigs

EXAMPLE 2

<u>Apuñalaron a un cliente</u>
Cuatro niños atracan un banco en Valencia
Valencia/E.P.

Cuatro niños de edades comprendidas entre 12 y 16 años atracaron en la mañana del lunes una sucursal de la Caja de Ahorros de Valencia. Los menores irrumpieron en el banco armados con varias navajas, con las que amenazaron a los empleados y clientes. Tras apoderarse de ciento veinte mil pesetas, un cliente les hizo frentes, siendo agredido con una navaja por uno de los menores, que le provocó heridas de gravedad.

Cuando los asaltantes intentaban escapar, los empleados de la sucursal bancaria bloquearon las puertas del local y consiguieron que uno de los niños quedara retenido entre las puertas de entrada y de salida, donde fue detenido poco después, al igual que los otros tres menores, que fueron capturados en las inmediaciones de la sucursal.

(Ya, 9.3.88)

Choose the correct answer for each of the following:

1. Los jóvenes atracaron el banco
   (a) entre mediodía y las cuatro de la tarde
   (b) armados con navajas
   (c) amenazando a los empleados con una escopeta
   (d) sin violencia

2. Uno de los niños
   (a) hizo frente a un empleado
   (b) se sentó cerca de la puerta de entrada
   (c) asaltó al cliente que no quería seguir sus órdenes
   (d) se cayó

3. Los empleados de banco
   (a) bloquearon las puertas de la sucursal
   (b) intentaron escapar
   (c) asaltaron a los atracadores
   (d) escaparon a la calle

4. Robaron
   (a) 12.000 ptas.
   (b) 20.000 ptas.
   (c) 200.000 ptas.
   (d) 120.000 ptas.

5. Después capturaron
   (a) a tres heridos
   (b) a uno de los niños
   (c) a los cuatro atracadores
   (d) a tres niños de la localidad

EXAMPLE 3

Skandalöser Giftgas-Unfall brachte Altenheimbewohner in tödliche Gefahr
Weil ein Angestellter schlampte, wurden 13 pflegebedürftige Frauen und Männer Opfer des Unglücks

"Es war schrecklich", erinnert sich die 71jährige Adelheid Stury, Bewohnerin des Münchner Hans-Sieber-Altenheims. "Ich habe kaum noch Luft bekommen können und glaubte, jeden Moment elend ersticken zu müssen."

Auch ihre Zimmernachbarin Julia Denk (81) überkommt heute noch Angst, wenn sie an jenes Ereignis zurückdenkt, das sie fast das Leben gekostet hätte. "Todesangst habe ich gehabt", sagt die alte Dame. "Eine Angst, wie ich sie meinem ärgsten Feind nicht wünsche."

Ån einem Montag war es passiert. Karl Mayerhofer, Leiter der Bade- und Therapie-Abteilung des Seniorenheims, in dem rund 300 alte Menschen leben, hatte gerade eine Patientin im Sitzstuhl ins Schwimmbecken gelassen, als er einen übel stechenden Gasgeruch bemerkte.

"Ich wusste sofort, dass es sich um Chlorgas handelte", erzählt der 42jährige Bademeister. Keuchend lief Karl Mayerhofer in die Anmeldung der Badeabteilung und alarmierte sofort Heimleiter Bertram Gruber. Der rief Polizei und Feuerwehr an und trommelte über Funk sämtliche Mitarbeiter zusammen.

"Wir hatten gerade zu Mittag gegessen", erinnert er sich. "Einige unserer alten Leute machten ihren Mittagsschlaf. Ausserdem haben wir natürlich auch einige Pflegefälle im Heim. Unvorstellbar, was passiert wäre, wenn sich das Gas durch alle Räume ausgebreitet hätte."

Umgehend liess Bertram Gruber die bettlägerigen Patienten evakuieren. Diejenigen Senioren, die sich zum Mittagsschlaf hingelegt hatten, wurden geweckt und in Sicherheit gebracht - einige konnten alleine gehen, andere wurden in Rollstühle gesetzt oder mit ihren Betten ins Freie geschoben.

Einer der Bewohner berichtet: "Nur der Geistesgegenwart von Herrn Mayerhofer und Herrn Gruber sowie dem Einsatz der übrigen Helfer ist zu verdanken, dass es nicht zu einer grossen Katastrophe kam."

Dennoch: 13 pflegebedürftige Frauen und Männer mussten mit zum Teil schweren Chlorgasvergiftungen ins Krankenhaus eingeliefert werden. Bleibende Schäden aber befürchten die Ärzte bei keinem von ihnen.

Ausgelöst wurde der skandalöse Giftgasunfall durch die Schlamperei eines 47jährigen Heizungsarbeiters. "Obwohl im Heizungsraum grosse Hinweisschilder vor der Gefahr warnen", sagt Bademeister Mayerhofer, "hat er einfach Salzsäure in die Reinigungsmaschinen des Schwimmbeckens gefüllt. Sofort bildete sich hochgiftiges Chlorgas, das über Liftschächte ins ganze Haus zog."

(*Neue Post*, 24.7.87)

Open questions in English

Answer the following questions:
1. Who was the first to notice that there was something wrong?
2. What attracted his attention?
3. What was he doing at the time?
4. What was his immediate reaction?
5. What did the director of the old folks' home do?
6. At what time of day did the accident happen?
7. How did the personnel and other helpers evacuate the old people? What did they have to do first?
8. How many people needed hospital treatment?
9. Who caused the accident? Where did the poisonous gas come from?
10. How did it seep into the building?

EXAMPLE 4

Des Weihnachtsmannes Domizil

Der Weihnachtsmann, der ja schon eine Wohnung beispielsweise in North Pole in Alaska und an einigen anderen Orten auf der Welt hat, besitzt auch in Finnland ein festes Domizil. Von den Fremdenverkehrsbehörden ist ihm dieses zwar nicht am Nordpol, aber doch nahe am Polarkreis, in Rovaniemi, zugewiesen worden, rund 2500 Kilometer vom nördlichsten Punkt der Erde entfernt. Und ausgestattet ist dieses Domizil mit Werkstätte und einer Kurzwellenradiostation, alles in der Hoffnung, dass dies Touristen aus aller Welt in den hohen Norden Finnlands locken könne. Um für sich selbst und für Finnland zu werben ist der finnische Nikolaus schon weit gereist, nach Los Angeles und Singapur beispielsweise. Und aus der Schweiz hat er schon 20, aus Beverly Hills in Kalifornien 50 Kinder nach Rovaniemi geholt, damit sie sich seinen Wohnsitz mit eigenen Augen anschauen konnten.

Sein «Reich» ist ein rund 112 000 Quadratkilometer grosses Stück arktischer Wildnis, in dem neben mehr als 300 000 Rentieren auch knapp 200 000 Menschen leben. Die amtliche Adresse des Weihnachtsmannes lautet: 99999 Korvatunturi, Finnland. Er selbst oder einer seiner Helfer werde jeden Brief beantworten, der einen Absender trage, wird versichert. Ein internationales Unternehmen hat ihm einen Computer gestiftet, damit er es leichter hat, die rund 200 000 Briefe zu beantworten, die ihm dieses Jahr

Kinder aus 90 Ländern geschrieben haben. Amateurfunker können den Weihnachtsmann angeblich unter dem Rufzeichen OH9SCL erreichen.

(*Basler Zeitung*, 24.12.86)

Open questions in target language

Lies den Artikel und beantworte die folgenden Fragen:
1. Wo wohnt der finnische Weihnachtsmann?
2. Wie weit ist seine Wohnung vom Nordpol entfernt?
3. Wie gross ist sein Reich? Wieviele Menschen wohnen dort?
4. Wie lautet die Adresse?
5. Wieviele Briefe hat der Weihnachtsmann im letzten Jahr bekommen? Aus wievielen verschiedenen Ländern?
6. Wie kann man den Weihnachtsmann auch noch erreichen, per Funk oder per Telefon? Wie lautet die Nummer?

Examples 1-4 discussed

In the sense that it does not require learners to formulate answers, whether in English or the target language, the multiple-choice format used in Examples 1 and 2 is clearly easier to deal with than the open-question format used in Examples 3 and 4. Example 1 draws attention to the fact that in devising multiple-choice questions it is not always easy to find plausible alternatives. However, although this is a serious matter in an examination or test, it is much less serious in an exercise designed for use in the clasroom.

Difficulty of task related to question types and whether or not questions are in target language

How is the difficulty of the task affected by the language in which the questions are put? Questions in English require learners to be able in some sense to translate from English to the target language and back again; and they are likely to offer very little help in unlocking those parts of the target language text that are opaque to them. Questions in the target language, on the other hand, may actually help learners to understand the text better; though they may also encourage them to tackle the task by a process of word-identification that involves a minimum of comprehension. This is especially true of the multiple-choice format. Open questions in the target language require not only comprehension but production, and in some cases may presuppose a relatively sophisticated competence; in other words, Example 4 is potentially a much more difficult task to accomplish well than Examples 1-3.

In principle comprehension questions can provide the learner with a "comprehension frame", that is, a preliminary

38

outline of the thematic structure of the text - the more questions there are, the more likely they are to benefit the learner in this way. Thus work on the questions *before* the text is read can do much to facilitate comprehension. However, the other side of this coin is that the questions inevitably impose one particular focus on the text and thus may limit the learner's approach to it.

Whatever their virtues as test types, exercises of the kind exemplified in Examples 1-4 have a limited capacity to promote interactive language learning. For one thing they constrain the learners' approach to the authentic text and virtually ensure that much will be left out of account; for another they have only limited usefulness as the focus for group or pair work - two heads may well be better than one, but the nature of the activity is not guaranteed to promote the negotiation of meaning in the target language which is the basis of communicative learning. What is more, exercises of this kind take quite a lot of time and effort to devise, which is appropriate to a question on a public examination paper but not necessarily to a learning activity that will occupy a class for perhaps half a lesson.

Example 5 offers an interesting variant on the traditional comprehension exercise: if these are the answers, what are the questions?

EXAMPLE 5

Seat entrega Málaga 100.000
Seat ha fabricado y vendido ya más de cien mil unidades de su modelo Málaga, que tan buena acogida tiene tanto en el mercado español como en los mercados exteriores.

El fabricante hispano que exporta en estos momentos a treinta países tiene previsto cerrar el presente ejercicio con más de 155.000 millones de pesetas de facturación en concepto de ventas al exterior.

(*El Independiente*, 5.12.87)

Here is a comprehension exercise with a difference. Instead of having to answer questions, you are given the answers and have to supply appropriate questions.

1. ¿...........................?
    Una compañía que fabrica automóviles.
2. ¿...........................?
    Cien mil.
3. ¿...........................?
    Sí, tanto en España como en el extranjero.
4. ¿...........................?
    Treinta países.
5. ¿...........................?
    155.000 millones de pesetas.

Although it requires the same level of competence in the target language as Example 4, Example 5 may by its very unusualness involve the learner in a less constrained interaction with the target language text than a traditional comprehension exercise. And its reversal of expected procedures begins to suggest a means of exploiting traditional comprehension exercises in a manner more likely to involve learners in interaction both with one another and with the target language. We made the point above that devising

exercises of this kind is a time-consuming activity; but the time will be well spent if it is the learners themselves who devise the exercise. It is possible to envisage an activity that begins by asking each learner to devise five comprehension questions for homework; continues by putting learners in groups to construct a finished exercise; and ends by having the groups exchange and compare exercises.

(ii) Comprehension by evaluation of content

Concern that traditional approaches to teaching comprehension were insufficiently interactive was doubtless one of the considerations that led to the development of exercise types that approach comprehension rather more indirectly. Our next three examples all require learners to evaluate the

content of the text in one way or another. In Example 6 they have to decide whether a number of statements about Madonna are true or false; in Example 7 they have to decide which elements of the report about Charlie Nicholas are positive and which negative; and in Example 8 they have to extract from the text two lists of words and phrases, one concerned with victory and the other concerned with defeat.

EXAMPLE 6

La nouvelle Madonna

Seuls les beatles étaient arrivés à un tel résultat, dans les années soixante, mais Madonna a pulvérisé leur record. Une sacrée revanche pour la petite inconnue arrivée à New York en 1978 avec quelques dollars en poche, depuis son Michigan natal, et qui peut se vanter, à présent, d'être la seule chanteuse à avoir été cinq fois numéro un des ventes aux Etats-Unis au cours des cinq dernières années. En ce moment, Madonna, longtemps dénigrée par la presse de son pays, fait la une de bien des journaux. Elle a eu droit à la couverture de *Cosmopolitan*, et pour la première fois depuis un bon bout de temps, elle s'est confiée à plusieurs journalistes. Il faut dire qu'elle n'est pas très disponible, vu le planning imposé par le tour qui l'a entraînée des Etats-Unis jusqu'au Japon, en attendant l'Europe. Partout, le public a été frappé par sa transformation physique. Ella a perdu plusieurs kilos et arbore une ligne absolument superbe. Cette métamorphose, elle la doit à un changement radical d'alimentation. Madonna est végétarienne, et elle se contente, par exemple, à l'heure du déjeuner, d'un verre de lait de soja, d'une pomme et de chips de riz.

En ce moment, on parle encore de divorce entre Madonna et Sean Penn. L'intéressée est muette sur le sujet. On ne peut savoir ce qui sera passé entre le moment où cet article a été écrit et sa publication, mais une chose est certaine: les Penn ont chacun une personnalité explosive, et il est normal qu'il y ait souvent des étincelles entre eux. Cela dit, quand Madonna parle de celui pour qui elle eut le coup de foudre, dès leur première rencontre, elle dit des choses très tendres. Vous voulez une preuve? Madonna a horreur des chiens. Elle ne les supporte pas. En revanche, Sean les adore. Pendant le tournage du nouveau film de Madonna, «Who's that girl», le coiffeur de Griffin Dunne, le partenaire de Madonna, est arrivé un jour sur le plateau avec la photo de sa chienne et des petits qu'elle venait d'avoir. Qu'a fait Madonna? Elle est allée chercher l'un des chiots puis elle est rentrée jusqu'à sa villa. Là, elle a laissé l'animal devant la porte, puis elle a dit negligemment à Sean, qui était dans la maison: «Tu devrais aller dehors. Il y a quelqu'un qui voidrait faire ta connaissance». Quand Sean Penn a vu qui l'attendait, Madonna dit que son mari a été à deux doigts de se mettre à pleurer. Et après ça on dira que ces deux-là ne s'aiment pas! A d'autres ... D'autant plus que cette adoption représentait pour Madonna un véritable sacrifice. Elle ne regrette rien, car Sean est fou de son chien. «Et en plus, avoue Madonna en riant, j'ai choisi un de ces chiens qui deviennent aussi grands et costauds qu'un ours! Moi qui ne voulait pas d'un animal qui perd des poils sur les coussins ...» Elle sait être

41

vraiment touchante, Madonna. Ses problèmes avec son père, elle a aussi fini par les résoudre. Depuis l'enfance, elle lui en voulait, à ce père qui n'avait attendu que deux ans pour se remarier, alors que sa première femme - la mère de Madonna - était morte d'un cancer. Madonna n'avait que six ans quand elle perdit sa mère. «Je crois que c'est ce chagrin qui m'a donné l'envie de devenir quelqu'un, de me battre.» C'est aussi pourquoi elle a voulu régler ses comptes avec ce père qui ne la comprenait pas, lorsqu'elle chanta «Papa don't preach».

Il ne reste plus à Madonna qu'à faire la conquête de Paris, et le monde entier sera à ses pieds.

(Podium Hit, 9.87)

Ten statements, some true and some false, to be evaluated on the basis of the authentic text

Lisez l'article sur Madonna et marquez VRAI ou FAUX pour chaque phrase.

1. Madonna vient d'ajouter un nouveau disque à son palmarès.
2. A son arrivée à New York en 1978, Madonna était bien connue du public.
3. Elle a décidé de parler à la presse pour la première fois depuis longtemps.
4. Madonna a maigri grâce à un changement de régime.
5. Madonna parle beaucoup des bruits qui courent sur son divorce possible d'avec son mari Sean Penn.
6. Madonna aime bien les gros chiens.
7. Madonna a fait cadeau d'un tout petit chien à Sean Penn.
8. Sean Penn a été vraiment touché.
9. Madonna ne s'entend toujours pas avec son père.
10. Madonna était très heureuse avec son père dans son enfance.

EXAMPLE 7

Très cher Nicholas!
Après Hoddle et Hateley, un troisième britannique sur la Côte?

Placé sur la liste des transferts par Arsenal, Charlie Nicholas a déclaré qu'il souhaitait venir tenter sa chance en France: «Depuis que j'ai découvert le football français lors des deux dernières Coupes du monde je pense sincèrement que mon style de jeu est taillé sur mesure pour la France.»

Toulon qui est à la recherche d'un attaquant s'est aussitôt intéressé à l'Ecossais. C'est ce que nous a confirmé Rolland Courbis, l'entraîneur des Varois: «Nicholas fait effectivement partie des trois ou quatre joueurs avec qui nous sommes en contact. Tous appartiennent à la CEE. Aucune décision ne sera prise avant le 8 octobre au lendemain de Toulon-Laval (1).»

Nicholas a été écarté de l'équipe pro par George Graham l'entraîneur des «Gunners» pour insuffisance de performances et est proposé «à la vente» pour 6 millions de francs. Une somme qui fait tiquer le SC Toulon et Rolland Courbis!

Nicholas était arrivé à Arsenal voilà quatre ans. Le club londonien avait dû débourser 7,5 millions de francs pour obtenir sa signature. Le Celtic de Glasgow auquel appartenait Charlie est aujourd'hui disposé à le récupérer, mais préfère attendre, espérant qu'Arsenal sera contraint de baisser ses prétentions.

Nicholas qui vient de signer pour quatre années supplémentaires avec Arsenal évolue désormais avec l'équipe réserve. Où, paraît-il, ses prestations sont d'une rare médiocrité. Inutile de préciser que du côté des dirigeants londoniens on regrette amèrement d'avoir prolongé le contrat de l'Ecossais. Mais on se souvient qu'en fin de saison dernière il avait permis aux Gunners de remporter la Littlewood's Cup en marquant un but et en réussissant une passe décisive.

Soutenu par le public de Highbury qui apprécie son jeu spectaculaire, Nicholas s'était vu offrir un contrat juteux puisque son salaire est fixé à 80 000 francs par mois. Ce qui en Angleterre est exceptionnel! Reste à savoir si l'Ecossais qui évolue plutôt milieu offensif qu'attaquant de pointe est le joueur qui correspond à ce que recherche le S-G Toulon!   C.B.

(1) Courbis nous a confirmé qu'il n'était pas question que Bosman devienne Toulonnais cette saison, démentant ainsi certaines informations indiquant que le Hollandais pourrait signer à Toulon dès cette semaine.

(L'Equipe, 26-27.9.87)

Charlie Nicholas est un joueur de football à vendre. L'équipe de Toulon s'y intéresse. Pouvez-vous les aider à prendre une décision? Commencez en remplissant les cases ci-dessous.

éléments positifs	éléments négatifs

EXAMPLE 8

Le forcené de la Tour

Cet homme exténué dans les escaliers de la tour Eiffel est un Américain de trente-neuf ans, Steve Silva. Il a tenté en vain, samedi, de battre ce que le *Livre Guinness des records* appelle le "mile vertical", c'est à dire sept fois et demi la hauteur de la tour Eiffel. Pour battre le record, Steve Silva devait monter et descendre les 1 792 marches de la tour en 2 h 1'34". Il a finalement échoué de quatre-vingt-dix secondes.

(L'Equipe, 5.10.87)

Swing champion
Au début du tournoi la foule ne le connaissait que sous l'appella-
tion du "petit rouquin qui en veut". En trois jours *Ian Woosnam*
prouvait qu'on pouvait ne mesurer que 1,64 m et être le plus fort.
Non seulement le vainqueur du Trophée Lancôme écrasant tous
ces champions immenses, irlandais, écossais, allemands, améri-
cains, sud-africains, sans compter le plus fameux de tous, l'es-
pagnol Ballesteros, mais désormais classé numéro un européen!
Un titre qui lui a rapporté, à Saint-Nom, 500 000 francs, mais qui
ne lui suffit pas. C'est numéro un mondial qu'il veut désormais
être. Et dire qu'il y a quelques années à peine, le Gallois hésitant
entre la petite balle et le ballon rond ...

(L'Equipe, 3-4.10.87)

Specific elements to be extracted from authentic texts

Lisez les deux textes. Faites un liste des éléments linguistiques qui
illustrent la victoire et de ceux qui illustrent la défaite.

Discussion of Examples 6-8

Like the more traditional comprehension exercises,
Example 6 belongs to a kind that learners could well devise
themselves, using the procedures outlined above. Examples
7 and 8 lend themselves less obviously to this treatment, but
they have in their favour that they require very little preparation on the part of the teacher. They belong to a class of
activity that is easy to devise and organize and can lead to a
high level of interaction. For example, one can get the
learners to work in groups scanning a single text, a page of
texts, or a whole newspaper looking for good news and bad
The beginnings of an authentic response news. The very fact that they are asked to evaluate the
content of authentic texts in one way or another, involves
learners' affective faculties and is thus calculated to lead
them to at least the beginnings of an authentic response.

(iii) Information extraction

Comprehension as information extraction: Example 9 Closely related to the activities we have just been
considering are those that approach comprehension as a
matter of extracting information from the authentic text.
Thus Example 9 requires the learner to extract from a text
about Christopher Lambert information that might be used
in a "wanted" poster:

EXAMPLE 9

Er flog aus vier Schulen

"Er ist ein Typ, der sein Leben in seine Hände genommen hat. Ein Rebell, der sich gegen die drei Mächte in Sizilien auflehnte: die Kirche, den Adel, die Mafia. Er machte seinen Weg, er kämpfte gegen die Ungerechtigkeiten. Er war einer, der immer die Verantwortung für seine Taten übernahm, und er war auch ein grosser Romantiker, sehr idealistisch."

So beschreibt der 30jährige Christopher Lambert den gefürchtesten, bei den Armen des Landes aber auch verehrtesten Banditen Siziliens, Salvatore Giuliano. Lambert ist Giuliano in dem Action-Streifen "Der Sizilianer".

Christopher, der sich privat sehr lässig kleidet (meist Cordhose und Lederjacke), sucht nach seiner Brille. Er ist extrem kurzsichtig. "In meinen Filmen trage ich Haftschalen."

Christopher (in seiner Wahlheimat Frankreich schreibt er sich übrigens ohne r am Schluss) kam in New York zur Welt. Sein Vater war damals Diplomat bei den Vereinten Nationen und wechselte oft den Wohnort. Als Christopher ein Jahr alt war, zogen seine Eltern mit ihm nach Genf. Dort ging er auch zur Schule.

Christopher: "Ich war ein verdammt zerstreuter Schüler. Hatte nur Streiche im Sinn. Ich bin insgesamt von vier Schulen geflogen. Mein Vater war richtig sauer."

Nach dem Abitur (Christopher: "In den letzten Schuljahren habe ich wie ein Wilder gebüffelt") leistete er in Grenoble seinen Militärdienst bei den Alpenjägern ab. Anschliessend trat er als Praktikant in eine Bank in London ein. Dieser Job war ihm zu langweilig. Er ging nach Paris und wurde am Konservatorium zugelassen.

1980 drehte er seinen ersten Film "Le Bar du Telephone". Drei Jahre später ist er Tarzan in "Greystoke - Die Legende von Tarzan, Herr der Affen". Er wird ein Star. Weitere Filme: "Duett zu dritt", "Subway", "Highlander" und "I love you".

Privat ist Christopher mit der bildhübschen Schauspielerin Diane Lane ("Hautnah") heftig verbandelt.

(*Bravo*, 5.87)

Write a "wanted" poster based on information contained in the authentic text

Schreiben Sie einen "Steckbrief" für Christopher Lambert:

Name:
Alter:
Geburtsort:
Nationalität
Eltern (Beruf):
Schulbildung:

Militärdienst:
Ausbildung:
Filme:
Besondere Kennzeichen:

Other types of
information
extraction
exercise There are many possible variants on this approach to comprehension. For example, learners can work individually, in pairs, or in groups, filling out grids that analyse a single text or a whole page of a newspaper in terms of WHO?, WHAT?, WHEN? and WHERE? The same approach can be used to compare two or more reports of the same event or descriptions of the same person or place. Like activities that require an evaluative response from the learner, this kind of activity can lead to highly stimulating interaction; and once again it requires little preparation on the part of the teacher.

A further
variant Example 10 illustrates a rather different kind of activity that depends on extracting information from the authentic text: one newspaper report is used as the basis for re-ordering a jumbled version of another report of the same event.

EXAMPLE 10

<u>Veinte heridos</u>
Siete muertos en un accidente de tráfico por colisión de una moto y un autobús
IBIZA. - Una colisión frontal entre una moto de 850 centímetros cúbicos y un autocar con treinta y cinco turistas alemanes produjo ayer siete muertos y 20 heridos en Ibiza.

De los heridos, ocho con graves quemaduras fueron evacuados en helicóptero al hospital de la Fe de Valencia, según informó la Guardia Civil de Tráfico. En este centro sanitario se dispone de una unidad especial para este tipo de heridos. Todos ellos se encuentran en estado muy grave con quemaduras muy importantes.

El accidente se produjo a las 13,30 en el kilómetro 6,500 de la carretera entre Ibiza y Portinatx, en el término municipal de Santa Eulalia del Río.

Al parecer la colisión se produjo cuando la moto, marca *Guzzi*, adelantó a un vehículo y se empotró en el autocar.

(*En Diario 16*, 8.10.87)

46

Learners
restore order
to a jumbled
version of
another report
of the event
dealt with in the
authentic text

Use the above article to put the following pieces of a report of the
same event in the right order:

Una colisión frontal entre una moto de 850 centímetros cúbicos
y un autocar con turistas alemanes, algunos de los cuales regre-
saban hoy,

De éstos, ocho permancen graves, con quemaduras de consid-
eración en su cuerpo, en el hospital de La Fe, de Valencia,

Ibiza y Portinatx, comarcal 733, en el término municipal de Santa
Eulalia del Río.

provocando el incendio del autobús en el que viajaban treinta y
cinco turistas de nacionalidad alemana, seis de los cuales tam-
bién fallecieron.

adonde fueron evacuados en helicóptero y aviocar, por contar
con una unidad especial para este tipo de heridos.

Al parecer, la colisión se produjo cuando la moto Guzzi de gran
clindrada adelantó
De resultas de la violenta colisión, el conductor de la moto, al
parecer de nacionalidad italiana, resultó muerto en el acto y el
depósito de gasolina de la motocicleta estalló,

a un vehículo y se empotró en el autocar.

iban dos ocupantes.

El accidente se produjo a la una y media de la tarde de ayer en
el kilómetro 6,500 de la carretera entre

jueves, a su país de origen tras las vacaciones, produjo ayer siete
muertos y más de una veintena de heridos.

Noticias no confirmadas indican que en la moto

Once you have put these pieces together, compare the information
provided in the two articles under the headings TIME, LOCATION,
HOW THE ACCIDENT HAPPENED, NUMBER OF VICTIMS,
VEHICLES INVOLVED.

3.3 From production to reception

"Horizontal" and "vertical" structures

In Chapter 2 we suggested that what we called "horizontal structures", the morpho-syntactic forms of a language, are acquired within a framework of "vertical structures" established by knowledge of the norms of interaction (see p.27 above). Of course, as we noted in Chapter 1, all learning is a matter of integrating new knowledge with what we already know, and the comprehension exercises we have illustrated in 3.2 all presuppose a fair degree of linguistic knowledge. They are organized in such a way that the learner is unable to exploit his world knowledge unless he possesses a minimum of grammatical, lexical and discourse knowledge; and this means that they have limited potential for language *learning* as opposed to language *practice*. It is difficult to use them successfully in the early stages of learning. If the learner is to begin to derive from his diet of authentic texts the benefits claimed in Chapters 1 and 2, we must devise ways of activating his world and discourse knowledge while at the same time compensating for deficiencies in his linguistic (grammatical and lexical) knowledge.

(i) Predictive activities

One way of activating learners' world and discourse knowledge is to involve them in predictive activities of the kind illustrated in Example 11.

EXAMPLE 11

Before reading the article printed below, see if you can work out the order in which these events occurred:
- El yate salió el jueves.
- Hubo un fallo del compás.
- El yate volvió el lunes.
- Iban a hacer unas compras.
- El jueves por la noche iniciaron el regreso.
- Salió para Fuerteventura.
- Las autoridades de Marina iniciaron las operaciones
- Debía volver el viernes.
- Salió desde Las Palmas.

Write out the sentences in the correct order. You will find that you have a story that needs to be tidied up. Try to do this by cutting out

Read the authentic text

any unnecessary repetition and adding any necessary connectors. Now read the text printed below and compare the story it tells with your own story.

Las Palmas de Gran Canaria
Regresó a puerto un yate tras haber sido dado por desaparecido

Un yate, que salió el jueves desde Las Palmas para el sur de Fuerteventura, a donde tenía que haber llegado el viernes, y que fue dado por desaparecido anteayer, regresó ayer a Gran Canaria.

Según declaró a la agencia Efe su propietario y patrón, Miguel Angel Ramos Mendoza, «todo se debió» a un fallo del compás que les daba un «rumbo falso» y que los acercó, «casi, a la costa africana».

Se trata del yate «Dachkaesfchawdag», de 9 metros de eslora, adquirido en Fuerteventura, concretamente en Morro Jable, por Ramos Mendoza a un alemán y que lo dedica a su uso particular.

El miércoles día 8, Ramos Mendoza, su compañera y sus dos pequeños hijos, decidieron venir desde Fuerteventura a Las Palmas para hacer unas compras «porque aquí las cosas están más baratas».

El jueves por la noche iniciaron el regreso, llevando como «invitado» a un joven, pariente de un amigo de la pareja, que pretendía buscar trabajo en la zona turística de Fuerteventura.

En una travesía normal, la embarcación debía haber llegado en la mañana del viernes a Morro Jable, y no lo hizo.

No obstante, quienes esperaban al joven invitado en Fuerteventura empezaron a inquietarse hasta el punto de denunciar la «desaparición» del yate a las autoridades de Marina en la tarde del domingo.

Las autoridades de Marina de Gran Canaria y Fuerteventura iniciaron las operaciones de búsqueda del yate en las costas de estas islas, con resultado negativo.

Cuando en la mañana de ayer la Comandancia de Marina iba a solicitar los servicios de un avión del SAR se advirtió, en el muelle deportivo, la presencia del yate que, según el celador de la Junta del Puerto, entró de madrugada.

Ramos Mendoza explicó que «todo se debió» a un «rumbo falso» que le daba el compás del yate, que los alejó más de la cuenta del rumbo previsto para dirigirse al sur de Fuerteventura.

(*Diario de Cadiz*, 14.7.87)

Example 11 is based on the belief that the process of ordering the nine sentences will activate learners' knowledge of the sea, boats and accidents, and that this will facilitate their comprehension of the authentic report of an accident at sea. When they read the authentic text they cannot help but match it against the target-language scenario they have already constructed. What is more, this process should also facilitate learning, since new material is being presented within a fully elaborated context of meaning, thus making it easier for learners to associate new knowledge with what they already know.

Presenting
new material
within a fully
elaborated
context of
meaning

(ii) Organizing vocabulary

The processes involved in Example 11 may well lead to effective learning; but learners still need a fair degree of grammatical and (especially) lexical knowledge in order to attempt the exercise with anything approaching confidence. Of course, it is possible to overcome this difficulty by introducing the exercise with a brain-storming session on relevant vocabulary. Example 12 effectively does this, combining work on vocabulary with the creation of a scenario that will provide a framework within which to encounter and respond to the authentic text.

EXAMPLE 12

Preparatory
task: make up
a story from
a jumble of
phrases

Working in pairs or small groups, invent a story using as many as possible of the following phrases:

ambas de 25 años - tras tomar unas copas - dos mujeres que sirvieron de gancho - en la calle Valvrede de Madrid - le dejaron en libertad - la policía arrestó a las dos parejas - un cuarto de hora - según informa - robar dinero, ropa y un reloj - dos hombres - intimidaron al visitante - llevaron a cabo el asalto

Now read the following article and compare it with your own story.

Dos mujeres llevaron a un hombre a su casa para robarle
El País, **Madrid**

Dos mujeres que sirvieron de *gancho*, y otros dos hombres que llevaron a cabo el asalto, fueron detenidos ayer acusados de robar dinero, ropa y un reloj a un hombre de 46 años, según informa la Jefatura Superior de Policía de Madrid.

María Nieves Cabrera y Dolores Monge Guillén, ambas de 25 años, conocieron en la calle Valverde de Madrid a un hombre al que tras tomar unas copas con él, le llevaron a una casa de la barriada del Pozo del Huevo, en Entrevías. Cuando apenas llevaban un cuarto de hora en su interior, siempre de acuerdo con el relato policial, entraron en la casa Miguel Angel González Marcos, de 27, y Francisco Javier Melero Ballesteros, de 26, quienes intimidaron al visitante con un objeto contundente y al que robaron el reloj, una cazadora de cuero, un talonario de cheques y una tarjeta de crédito. Posteriormente le dejaron en libertad.

La policía, tras recibir la llamada del asaltado, hizo un rastreo por la zona y arrestó a las dos parejas, recuperando todo el botín.

(*El País*, 21.11.87)

(iii) Productive exercise chains

Examples 13 & 14 introduced

Examples 11 and 12 both involve learners in predictive activity that is productive in a limited way. Examples 13 and 14 take this a stage further and place the authentic text at the end of a chain of activities involving them in more fully elaborated productive activities.

EXAMPLE 13

Preparatory tasks: sort jumbled nouns and verbs into categories according to meaning ...

(a) Here is a jumble of VERBS and NOUNS:

Polizei - Taucher - liegen - finden - Diebstahl - Menge - Hotel - stehlen - hinunterhoppeln - Touristen - Auto - Grund des Rheins - prüfen - anziehen - Parkplatz - kommen - versinken - anrufen - Versicherung - zurückdrängen - Treppe -Kranwagen - Auto - Rheinufer - Zeuge - denken - hieven - Feuerwehr - Wagen - melden - Handbremse

Which verbs and nouns can be linked together?

...create a story from the combinations of nouns and verbs ...

(b) Try to create a story from your combinations of nouns and verbs. You will need to include information about WER?, WO?, WANN? and WAS?

(c) Re-order the following thirteen sentences to make an accident report:

... put jumbled sentences in order ...

- Der Wagen versank allmählich.
- Die Polizei und die Feuerwehr kamen zum Rheinufer.
- Zwei Taucher fanden das Auto.
- Das Paar sagte, sie hätten die Handbremse angezogen.
- Sie wollten den Diebstahl einem Polizisten melden.

51

- Der Polizist sagte, das Auto lag auf dem Grund des Rheins.
- Die Versicherung wird die Sache prüfen.
- Mit dem Kranwagen hievten sie das Auto aus dem Wasser.
- Sie drängten die Menge zurück.
- Der Zeuge lief zum Hotel, um die Polizei anzurufen.
- Sie dachten, es sei gestohlen.
- Ein Zeuge erzählte, dass das Auto die Treppe zum Rhein hinuntergehoppelt sei.
- Zwei Touristen kamen zum Parkplatz am Rheinufer zurück und fanden ihr Auto nicht mehr.

... edit story created from nouns and verbs

(d) Go back to your own story and edit it, paying particular attention to verb forms, agreement of nouns and adjectives, and word order.

Read authentic text

(e) Now read the following newspaper report:

Die Suche nach dem versunkenen Auto auf dem Rheingrund
Als das Paar aus Ahrweiler zum Parkplatz am Rheinufer zurückkehrte, war sein Auto verschwunden. Gestohlen sei es, dachten sie. Im selben Moment nahmen sie den Menschenauflauf an der Theodor-Heuss-Brücke wahr. Sprang dort ein Mensch in die Fluten, um sich das Leben zu nehmen? Die Wahrheit erfuhren die beiden Touristen wenige Minuten später von einem Polizisten, dem sie den Diebstahl melden wollten: das Auto aus Ahrweiler lag auf dem Grund des Rheins. Was war geschehen? Ein Augenzeuge berichtete, er habe auf der Treppe am Ufer gelesen, als es plötzlich neben ihm scheppterte. Im nächsten Augenblick hoppelte ein nagelneuer Citroën dem Rhein entgegen, Stufe für Stufe, mit viel Schwung. Niemand hätte ihn halten können.

Der Wagen tauchte zuerst mit dem Heck ins Wasser, trieb dann ab, schwamm eine Weile und versank allmählich. Gerade noch konnte der erschrockene Leser erkennen, dass niemand in dem Auto sass. Auch die Kennzeichen konnte er sich merken. Dann sprintete er in ein nahegelegenes Hotel, um die Polizei zu verständigen, ein Portier telefonierte für ihn, trotz anfänglicher Zweifel.

Am Ufer sammelte sich schnell eine Menge Schaulustiger, ebenso auf der Theodor-Heuss-Brücke. Polizei und Feuerwehr drängten die Leute am Ufer zur Seite, die Wasserschutzpolizei sperrte eine Spur des Fahrwassers. Zwei Segler zeigten die Stelle, an der sie den Citroën zuletzt sahen. Die beiden Taucher, Norbert Fuchs und Hans Keiner, stiegen über den Leiterwagen hinab in die Fluten. Binnen zwanzig Minuten, die wie eine

Ewigkeit wirkten, orteten sie das Auto und banden es fest. "Es lag 15 Meter entfernt aus vom Ufer in 3,50 m Tiefe", berichtete Norbert Fuchs später. Das Wasser war zu dem Zeitpunkt 22 Grad warm, die Strömung aber gewaltig wie stets. Mit Stahlseil und Seilwinde hievte die Feuerwehr den Wagen an die Oberfläche. Ölblasen quollen auf und zerplatzten zu kleinen, schillernden Teppichen. Der Kranwagen nahte, die Taucher banden zwei Schlaufen um das Auto. Kranfahrer Wilfried Jahres hob es behutsam an, Sturzbäche strömten aus dem Inneren des Citroëns. Doch halt! Der Wagen drohte aus den Laschen zu kippen. Kommando zurück, die gleiche Arbeit nochmals. Diesmal gelang es; die beiden Pechvögel aus Ahrweiler hatten ihr Auto wieder, durchnässt und verbeult. Sie trugen's mit Fassung.

Sie sagten, sie seien sicher, die Handbremse angezogen zu haben. Die Versicherung wird den Badeausflug des Autos prüfen, das abgeschleppt wurde. Ein Fremder fragte die beiden freundlich: "Kann ich Sie irgendwohin fahren?" Doch höflich lehnte das Paar ab.

(*Allgemeine Zeitung*, 21.9.87)

EXAMPLE 14

<table>
<tr><td>

Preparatory tasks:
sort a jumble
of nouns into
categories ...

</td><td>

(a) Ci-dessous une série de substantifs en vrac. Mettez-vous à trois ou quatre et arrangez les substantifs en plusieurs catégories.

le moteur - la mer - le corps - le hors-bord - le voilier - les copains - le mât - le port - les blessées - le propriétaire - un passager - l'hélice - le pilote - le pont

</td></tr>
<tr><td>

... make simple
sentences
using the above
nouns and these
verbs ...

</td><td>

(b) Faites des phrases simples à l'aide des substantifs cidessus et des verbes suivants:
avoir - fracasser - foncer - entendre - déchiqueter - voir - s'effondrer - masser - passer par-dessus bord

</td></tr>
<tr><td>

...write a simple
story outline

</td><td>

(c) Vous avez le titre: "Le hors-bord fracasse le voilier". Maintenant essayez de fabriquer une version simple du scénario de l'histoire.

</td></tr>
<tr><td>

Read the
authentic text
and use it
to correct or
improve the
story outline

</td><td>

(d) Lisez maintenant l'article suivant et corrigez ou améliorez votre scénario selon le cas.

</td></tr>
</table>

Chauffards de la mer, encore un drame
Le hors-bord fracasse le voilier: 2 morts, 4 blessés
Les six copains auraient décidé une sortie nocturne, et ils ont vu l'étrave sauvage leur foncer dessus.

53

Quand ils ont vu foncer droit sur eux le hors-bord fou, juste à sortie du port de Beaulieu, Véronique, Bernard, Thierry et trois copains, massés sur le pont de leur petit voilier, ont hurlé: «Mais arrêtez! Arrêtez!» Avec le grondement du moteur de 200 ch. le pilote du «Star-Galaxy» n'a ni entendu ni vu les signes de détresse. Le choc a littéralement fracassé le «Barbajacou» et projeté à la mer Pascal Manini, vingt-quatre ans, déchiqueté par l'hélice du bateau harponneur. Brisé net, le mât du voilier - un six mètres - s'est effondré sur un autre passager, Alex Vorelly, vingt-quatre ans, actuellement dans un état très critique. Dans le choc d'une violence inouïe, un jeune marin suédois du «Galaxy» est passé par-dessus bord. Son corps n'a été retrouvé qu'hier matin, par 16 mètres de fond.

«Il était 22 h 30. On venait de dîner sur le bateau, au port, et quelqu'un a eu l'idée d'une petite balade en mer, à la fraîche», raconte Bernard Sidler, l'un des rescapés miraculeusement indemne.

- On n'a pas vraiment eu le temps de se rendre compte», précise son copain Thierry Delettre, un jeune Parisien en vacances. «C'était à un mille à peine au large. On avait pourtant nos feux de position.» Excès de vitesse incontestable, grave faute d'inattention et manque de maîtrise de cette vedette rapide, annexe d'un yacht ancré à Saint-Jean-Cap-Ferrat, le «Galaxy». C'est son propriétaire, René Herzog, homme d'affaires suisse mais dont la société est à Londres, qui avait pris les commandes. A ses côtés, deux marins, un jeune Anglais, Nicholas Cuttelle, qui s'en tire sans une égratignure, et Robert Kirid, le Suédois.

Prévenus du drame par le sémaphore de Beaulieu, les secours s'organisaient très vite, mais il est trop tard pour Pascal Manini, employé de banque à Villefranche. Véronique Bolinowski, vingt et un ans, la seule fille du groupe, souffrant d'un hématome à la tête, et Pascal Panizzi, légèrement blessé à une main, n'étaient, eux, hospitalisés que quelques heures.

(*Le Parisien*, 21.8.87)

Discussion of Examples 13 and 14: having learners approach the authentic text via the creation of a text of their own

The technique of having learners approach an authentic text via the creation of a text of their own perhaps takes the deliberate activation of existing knowledge as far as it is useful to go. It is important to emphasize that this technique was devised to facilitate the twin processes of comprehension and learning and not as a new way of getting learners to write essays in the target language. In the first instance the texts that they produce must be judged for their usefulness as comprehension aids and not condemned as hopelessly deficient attempts at pastiche (this is not to say, of course, that a particularly promising scenario should not be further edited into a well-finished text in its own right).

This approach to the comprehension of authentic texts will be unfamiliar to many teachers, so it is worth considering two texts produced by learners on their way to reading an authentic text. The learners' texts clearly illustrate how their knowledge of the world and of how stories are written enabled them to free linguistic potential that might otherwise have gone unrecognized and unfulfilled. The first text is the work of four 13-year-old girls in their second year of learning French (the authentic text in question was about James Dean); the second was written by a 12-year-old boy in his first year of learning French (the authentic text was about an accident in a quarry).

Text produced by four 13-year-old girls

James Dean Septembre 1955: il habite en Bakersfield. Il aimé le cinema et à 24 ans il a allé en Californie et il entré le cinema. Il as très bien. Il ne porter pas uniforme, mais il preferè blue jeans et t-shirt. Les adolescents adorent James Dean et ses films, par example *A l'Est d'Eden* et *Geant.* Les années 80 le film *"La Fureur de Vivre"* tres populaire. 1987 dans le Ford Modèle 50 il a eu accident et il mouri. Il a eu trente-deux ans. Aujourd-hui il a symbole et célèbre salles de cinema et les adolescents et les adultes moderne aiment James Dean.

Text produced by 12-year-old boy

Hasard de mortel

Le Martine et Jean-Luc dans un caverne. Commencer un glisser et s'affaisser un caverne. "Il faut échapper" dire Martine. Voir homme vieux le glisser. "Il faut donner l'alerte" il dire. Arriver police. "Ils faut être mort" dire un. Enlever le police le glisser. Etre Martine et Jean-Luc être dans un état grave. Aller Jean-Luc et Martine hôpital. Ils être mort le Lendemain. Le lendemain être ensevelir.

Many teachers throw up their hands in horror at these texts because of the errors they contain. But if we disregard the errors we cannot but be amazed at the pupils' achievement in using minimal linguistic means to communicate very interesting accounts of, respectively, James Dean and an imagined accident. Both texts have a clear "vertical" structure, in the sense in which we used that term in Chapter 2, yet their "horizontal" structure is "pragmatic" rather than "syntactic". That is to say, it is made up of small rather than large chunks, which are articulated according to a topic-comment rather than a subject-predicate pattern; the relation between chunks is one of loose co-ordination rather than tight subordination; the ratio of nouns to verbs is low; and there is no use of morphology.

It is important to note that after they had composed their own texts these learners found the authentic text in question easy to understand, which they almost certainly would not have done if they had attempted to read it without this kind of preparation. What is more, we would argue that the technique illustrated here can greatly speed up the growth of the learner's interlanguage; and it is of course on a broadly based interlanguage that the development of more refined linguistic skills depends.

3.4 Productive activities

Although we have so far been concerned with exercises designed to promote learning through the comprehension of authentic texts, most of the examples we have given involve learners in some kind of productive activity, especially if the target language is predominantly the language of classroom management and instruction. This should warn us against assuming too rigid a division of the language skills according to exercise type. At the same time, the communicative competence that we want our learners to develop in interaction with authentic texts should include the capacity to go beyond reception to production, to give linguistic expression to their response to the authentic text. Thus it is entirely appropriate that we should want some of our learners' work with authentic texts to have oral or written production of the target language as its explicit goal.

In keeping with the general principles of our approach, we shall want our learners' productive activities to be authentic - concerned with the purposeful communication of meaning. Authenticity in this dimension is a particularly slippery concept. In order to do justice to the social reality of the target language on the one hand and our classroom on the other we should perhaps recognize two basic orders of authenticity. The first order has to do with the classroom as a place where learning takes place within a unique structure of social relationships; whereas the second order has to do with the target language community and the contexts in which our learners may use the target language when they are not in the classroom. Clearly, there are points at which the two orders of authenticity overlap - for example, in a well-realized role play based on spoken or written production. But there are also points at which learners may be involved in activities which are entirely authentic in terms of the first order but largely inauthentic in terms of the second - for example, when they write an essay in the target language; the point being that writing essays is an activity largely limited to classrooms and a very small class of journalists and professional writers. As far as the development of the learners' communicative competence is concerned, the two orders of authenticity must be held in careful balance. Learners need to learn how to behave in the target language community by practising some of the roles they are likely to be called on to play; at the same time the classroom can offer a whole range of activities that have no equivalent in the world outside but will help them to consolidate what they learn by other means.

The ability to speak and (more especially) write fluently in a foreign language is a very substantial achievement, and it is unlikely that learners will develop productive skills rapidly or easily. Perhaps the biggest single fault to be found with traditional approaches to the teaching of productive skills is that they provide learners with far too little assistance. The classic instance of this is the homework essay: in many instances the title is the only help that learners get, so that they are all too likely to work out what they want to say

Traditional
approaches
to teaching
productive
skills give
learners
inadequate
support

in English and then try to translate it into the target language - with predictable results. The great virtue of using authentic texts as the basis of productive exercises is that they provide learners with thematic, discourse, grammatical and lexical frameworks within which to work.

(i) Rewriting texts

Examples 15 & 16 introduced

Examples 15 and 16, both originally the culmination of exercise chains similar to those in Examples 13 and 14, require learners to rewrite an authentic text. It is for the individual learner or group of learners to determine how far to depart from the structures of the original. Since a large part of the justification for basing productive activities on authentic texts lies in the help such texts provide, it is

Encouraging learners to remain within the limits of their competence

sometimes sensible to encourage learners to remain as far as possible within the limits of what they are confident they can get right. In terms of both learning value and motivation, it is good for learners to attempt something simple in the knowledge that they will get it right.

EXAMPLE 15

FÉLIX LA CHATTE GLOBE-TROTTER

En vingt-neuf jours, une chatte a parcouru plus de 280 000 km! Elle a traversé trois continents. Pas à pattes, bien sûr, mais dans la soute d'un avion de la Panam, où elle se trouvait incognito.

A l'origine, la chatte, qui se nomme Félix, devait arriver le 3 décembre à l'aéroport de Los Angeles (Etats-Unis), après avoir fait le voyage avec sa maîtresse, Janice Kubecki, depuis Francfort. Mais sa cage avait été retrouvée vide. Finalement, Félix a été capturée dans le compartiment à bagages après plusieurs trajets. «Nous ne savons pas ce qu'elle a mangé», a déclaré un porte-parole de la compagnie, qui a écarté d'office la présence de souris clandestines dans l'avion.

Félix est maintenant en quarantaine à Londres, et attend que sa maîtresse revienne la chercher. En plus du voyage, elle devra rembourser les frais de procédure, qui se montent à 7 500 F.

(*Le Parisien*, 16-17.1.88)

Rewrite the authentic text, changing some of its central features

After a chain of activities similar to those in examples 13 and 14, comes the following:
Après avoir lu le texte, redigez un article intitulé "Le chien qui a parcouru l'Irlande".

58

EXAMPLE 16

Trempolino remporte l'Arc de Triomphe devant les anglais
Les bookmakers anglais n'ont vraiment pas de chance. Ils n'avaient que deux solutions perdantes dans l'Arc de Triomphe: ou le succès de REFERENCE POINT, grand favori de la course, sur lequel s'étaient abattues des pluies de livres sterling ces derniers jours, ou celui du français TREMPOLINO, monté par l'idole des petits turfistes britanniques, Pat Eddery, offert à 14/1. Débarrassés de bonne heure de REFERENCE POINT, ils devaient jubiler, mais leur joie a été de courte durée. Surgissant comme un diable de sa boite, leur bête noire TREMPOLINO s'envolait vers un succès évident ...

REFERENCE POINT, fidèle à son habitude, avait pris le train à son compte dès le départ, talonné par SHARANIYA qui avait manifestement pour mission de le faire sortir de ses gonds. NATROUN suivait tout près, suivi par ORBAN, TRIPTYCH, TABAYAAN, tandis que GROOM DANCER, TREMPOLINO et l'italien TONY BIN se désintéressaient le plus possible de la course. Avec où sans SHARANIYA, REFERENCE POINT se fût sans doute rendu de toute manière. Il l'a fait très tôt, peu après l'entrée de la ligne droite, et tous ceux qui l'avaient accompangé cédaient. TRIPTYCH elle même, la courageuse, la dure à cuire, demandait de l'oxygène.

A trois cent cinquante mètres du but, très intelligemment monté par Dominique Boeuf, GROOME DANCER tentait sa chance au meilleur endroit de la piste, le long du rail. Feu de paille. On sait maintenant qu'il ne tient pas, même par bon terrain. Simultanément, en pleine piste, TREMPOLINO trouvait facilement le passage, et accélérait en toute quiétude, vainement poursuivi par l'italien TONY BIN. Les attentistes avaient eu largement raison des plus impétueux. Il en va souvent ainsi à Longchamp dans les courses qui «roulent», comme disent les turfistes.

Pat Eddery remportait en l'occasion son quatrième Arc, égalant le record codétenu par Freddy Head, Yves Saint-Martin et Jacques Doyasbère. Mieux encore, il est le seul jockey à avoir remporté trois Arcs consécutifs (l'an passé DANCING BRAVE, il y a deux ans RAINBOW GUEST).

TREMPOLINO était le seul concurrent appartenant à un propriétaire français, ce qui n'a pu que réjouir le président de la République, venu hier aux courses pour la première fois de son septennat. François Mitterand a eu la chance de découvrir Longchamp par une belle journée d'automne, ce qui n'avait pas toujours été le cas pour ses prédécesseurs.

(*Le Matin*, 5.10.87)

Rewrite the
authentic text
so that the
race follows
a different
pattern from
the one reported

Parcourez le texte et notez la manière dont la participation de chaque cheval est décrite. Ensuite, lisez le text. Trempolino a gagné. Mais, imaginez que Reference Point ait gagné la course! A l'aide des phrases que vous avez déjà repérées dans le texte, décrivez cette course imaginaire. Essayez autant que possible de changer le rôle de la plupart des concurrents.

If undertaken with an appropriate degree of preparation, the act of editing or transposing an authentic text will involve learners in much analysis of the grammar of the original as well as its thematic and lexical content. In view of the importance that teachers and examiners traditionally

attach to grammatical and orthographical accuracy, it is rather odd that editing text has not been more widely recommended as a language learning technique. After all, it involves developing and practising precisely those skills on which accuracy of written production depends. The same skills are deployed in the correction of written work: the essential difference between learners on the one hand and teachers and examiners on the other is not that the latter have necessarily superior powers of invention, but that they have much more highly developed editing skills. This

provokes the thought that just as learners may profit more from devising than from answering traditional comprehension questions, so they may learn more from correcting one another's work than from looking through their own work after it has been corrected by the teacher.

(ii) Authentic texts and formal letters

Rewriting or transposing authentic texts is an activity that belongs firmly in the classroom, and thus to our first order of authenticity. Writing letters, on the other hand, is something that learners will need to do if they aspire to contact with their target language community; letter-writing thus belongs to our second order of authenticity.

Each language has its own conventions for the lay-out of letters, which can be particularly important in more formal communication. Learners need as part of their communicative survival kit a basic model of the formal letter that they can adapt to a variety of purposes. Example 17 provides

Example 17
introduced

such a model in German, the purpose of the authentic text (in this case a series of advertisements for summer courses) being to provide the learner with the pretext for writing the letter. The substance of the authentic text is included in the instructions given to the learner.

EXAMPLE 17

Schreibe einen Brief an die Kurverwaltung, 2242 Büsum. Bitte um Informationen zu dem Web- und Spinnkurs: Kosten, Daten, Übernachtung/Frühstück, Unterkunft, Anzahl der Stunden; bitte um eine Broschüre.

An die   .....
Kurverwaltung   .....
...   .
                                         den .....

Sehr geehrte/r ...,
Ich interessiere mich für ...
Könnten Sie mir bitte ...
Ich bedanke mich im Voraus für Ihre Mühe.

Mit freundlichen Grüssen
...

(iii) Authentic texts and personal letters

Personal letters differ from more formal correspondence in much the same way as casual, free-wheeling conversation differs from (say) a business meeting: to a considerable degree rhetorical structure is a matter of personal preference and tends to be much less important than content. Accordingly, once learners are in command of the basic conventions of letter-writing in their target language (lay-out, how to begin and end), they need help chiefly with content. Thus Example 18 is another exercise in text editing

Example 18
introduced

and transposition disguised as a letter-writing exercise; however, unlike Examples 15 and 16, the target text belongs to our second order of authenticity - it is a role play.

EXAMPLE 18

You are spending a week in the youth hostel in Wangerooge. Write a letter to your exchange partner in Hamburg describing Wangerooge, its youth hostel, and the things you do each day. Make as much use as you can of the material contained in the texts printed below.

WANGEROOGE

am Eingang zum Jadebusen ist die östlichste der Ostfriesischen Inseln. Ihre Geschichte ist sehr wechselvoll. Nachdem Wangerooge bereits 1327 Stadtrechte erhielt, lebten seine Bewohner bis zum Jahre 1818 mal unter russischer, niederländischer und französischer Herrschaft. Knapp 2000 Einwohner leben hier. Zu den Sehenswürdigkeiten der Insel gehört ein Naturschutzgebiet, Für den guten Rundblick bieten sich der Westturm und der Leuchtturm im Nordwesten der Insel an.

Bahnreise bis Sande, von dort mit dem Bus bis Harle zum Übergang aufs Schiff. Von Wangerooge Westanleger zum Ort fahren Sie mit der Inselbahn.

Deutsche Bundesbahn, Schiffsdienst und Inselbahn Wangerooge, 2944 Wittmund 2, Telefon: (0 44 69) 2 17.

Jugendherberge Wangerooge "Westturm"

Lage des Hauses: Der Turm - das Wahrzeichen Wangerooges - liegt am Westende der Insel und ist zu Fuss vom Anleger am Strand entlang in 20 Minuten zu erreichen. Bahnhof ist 45 Minuten entfernt.

Geeignet für: Einzelgäste, Ferienfreizeiten, Schulklassen, Schullandheimaufenthalte und Sportgruppen.

Freizeitangebote: Kirchen, Leuchtturm, Reitstall, Fahrradverleih und kulturelle Veranstaltungen. Um den Gästen reine Luft und Ruhe zu bieten, sind benzinbetriebene Fahrzeuge (mit Ausnahme von Krankenwagen und Feuerwehr) auf der Insel nicht gestattet. Möglichkeiten der Freizeitgestaltung: Führung ins Watt oder Vogelschutzgebiet, Krabbenkutterfahrt zu den Seehundsbänken, Nachbarinseln, evtl. Festland- sowie Helgolandfahrten, Fernsehen. Grillplatz am Haus. Ein bewachter Badestrand ist 200 m von der Jugendherberge entfernt.

Bankverbindung: Landeszentralbank Oldenburg, Zweigstelle Wangerooge Nr. 053-403 101, BLZ 280 501 00.

Nächste Jugendherbergen: Carolinensiel, Jever, Schillighörn.

Bitte beachten: Die Jugendherberge ist von Mai bis September geöffnet. Genauen Anfangs- und Schlusstermin bitte erfragen. Anreise nur nach Voranmeldung möglich. Der Aufenthalt ist kurtaxpflichtig und nur in Verbindung mit Vollverpflegung möglich. Träger Landesverband.

(iv) Curricula vitae

Letters apart, a *curriculum vitae* is perhaps the written text type that it is most useful for language learners to be able to produce. In all European cultures the *curriculum vitae* can take a number of forms, depending on the purpose it is intended to serve; these range from the extremely skeletal and schematic at one extreme to the discursive potted autobiography at the other. If they are provided with an appropriate model even learners in the earliest stages should be able to compile a *curriculum vitae* of the former kind - as instanced already in Example 9. Example 19 provides a further illustration.

EXAMPLE 19

Zwei Leben - ein Schicksal
44 Jahre wussten die Zwillinge Gerda Roleff und Erika Wagner gegenseitig nichts von ihrer Existenz. Jetzt trafen sie sich durch Zufall wieder. Und stellten trotz der langen Trennung verblüffende Gemeinsamkeiten fest. Bis hin zu ihren Kindern und Krankheiten.
Heute lachen sie über diese "dumme Sache". Und sehen sich mitten im Lächeln ernst an. Und sie sagen gleichzeitig und mit demselben Tonfall, jede das Echo der anderen: "Ein bisschen unheimlich ist das Ganze schon."

Die "dumme Sache" stiess den beiden Frauen zur gleichen Zeit zu: eine Blinddarmoperation.

Beide wussten damals nichts von der Existenz der anderen: Die eine lag in Berlin in der Klinik, die andere in Leipzig. Aber beide ärgerten sich: "Warum muss das ausgerechnet im Sommer passieren, wo alle Welt zum Baden geht?"

Zufall, dachte sich Erika Roleff in Berlin. Und in Leipzig tröstete sich Gerda Wagner: "Das ist eben Zufall ..."

Es war kein Zufall, sondern unbeeinflussbare Bestimmung. Eine Bestimmung, die beiden Frauen schon zum Zeitpunkt der Zeugung in jeder Körperzelle mitgegeben worden war. Erika Roleff und Gerda Wagner sind eineiige Zwillinge.

Aber das haben sie erst jetzt erfahren, nach 44 Jahren, als sie sich in Augsburg wiedertrafen. Aber diesmal wirklich durch einen Zufall ...

Die beiden wurden am 7. Juli 1939 als Gerda und Erika Wegener in Berlin-Karlshorst (heute DDR-Gebiet) geboren. Während der Bombennächte 1943 kam Gerda - damals vier Jahre alt - mit Lungenentzündung ins Krankenhaus. Wegen der Luftangriffe wurde sie eines Nachts Hals über Kopf mit allen anderen

Patienten nach Leipzig evakuiert.

Beim Transport ging das Namenbändchen an ihrem Handgelenk verloren.

Aus dem Krankenhaus kam die kleine Gerda in ein Leipziger Waisenhaus, später zu einer Pflegefamilie. 1978 zog sie nach Augsburg.

Ihre Zwillingsschwester Erika war mit den Eltern in Berlin geblieben. Verzweifelt suchten die Eltern jahrelang mit Hilfe des Roten Kreuzes, den Aufenthaltsort ihrer verschollenen Tochter Gerda zu finden. Ergebnislos.

Verständlich, dass sich Gerda bis zu dem zufälligen Treffen in Augsburg für eine Waise hielt. Denn erst jetzt, nach 44 Jahren, trat Zwillingsschwester Erika wieder in ihr Leben, als Gerda ein Pfund Kaffee kaufen wollte und in ein Geschäft in der Augsburger Innenstadt trat.

Die Kaffeeverkäuferin sprach sie sichtlich erfreut an: "Hallo, Tante Erika, wie geht's?" Gerda Wagner antwortete überrascht: "Was soll das? Ich kenne Sie nicht, ich bin nicht Ihre Tante."

Jetzt war die Verkäuferin, Lilo Wegner, 32, bestürzt. Wenn diese Frau, die genauso aussah und sprach wie ihre Tante Erika Roleff in Berlin, die sogar die gleiche Brille trug wie sie, nicht ihre Tante war - wer war sie dann? War diese Frau vielleicht die verschollene Zwillingsschwester?

So war es, so kam es zum Wiedersehen. Und dann feierten die Zwillinge. Mit einer Flasche Krimsekt. Und erzählten einander die Stationen ihrer getrennten Vergangenheit - zwei Schicksale mit erstaunlichen Übereinstimmungen.

Zuerst die Blinddarmoperation. Beide wie aus einem Mund: "Das war im Sommer 1962."

Erika: "1969 musste ich wieder ins Krankenhaus. Eine Operation an der rechten Brust ..."

Gerda zuckte zusammen: "Bei mir war 1969 das gleiche. Alles ging gut - aber jetzt plagen mich seit Jahren Migränenanfälle."

Erika: "So ein Zufall - mir geht's genauso."

Gerda brachte sieben Kinder zur Welt, auch Erika war siebenmal schawanger. Und noch mehr Gemeinsamkeiten. Beide tragen seit vielen Jahren die gleiche Kurzhaarfrisur, beide haben die gleichen Sehschwächen, beide tragen am liebsten Hosen und Pullis, beide lieben Operettenmusik.

Da sprach keine mehr von Zufall.

(*Quick*, 53/87)

Exercises in writing curricula vitae Complete this curriculum vitae:

Name: Erika Wegener

Geboren: 7. Juli ...

Geburtsort:

Aufgewachsen in:
Krankheiten:
im Alter von: ... Jahren
Kinder:

Now write a curriculum vitae for (a) Gerda and (b) yourself.

(v) Speaking activities

Speaking activities and the two orders of authenticity

Like the writing activities we have considered, speaking activities based on authentic texts can be categorized according to our two orders of authenticity. On the one hand there are activities that belong to the world of the classroom and form a continuum with the use of the target language as medium of classroom management and instruction; the learners' elicititation of one another's views, discussions, and debates fall into this category. On the other hand there are simulations that are focussed on one or another aspect of the target language culture - learners may, for example, act out roles suggested by the authentic text. It is fundamental to the whole argument of this book that learners will get more out of authentic texts the more thoroughly they are encouraged to interact with them. Speaking activities based on

The importance of appropriate preparation

authentic texts should be treated in the same way, which means that a discussion or role play is likely to succeed in proportion as it is thoroughly prepared - involving the learners in various kinds of lexical, grammatical, discourse and thematic analysis. Example 20 shows how an authentic

Example 20 introduced

text can be used to rehearse a conditional structure that is specially relevant to discussion of the theme "free time"; this is done not for its own sake, however, but as preparation for a class survey and discussion.

EXAMPLE 20

FREIZEIT

Alexandra ist in der Oper, Anja hat Probe, Dagmar gibt Turnunterricht und Manfred ist - wenn überhaupt - zwischen elf und zwölf zu erreichen. Nachts. Eines verbindet diese Teenager zwischen 15 und 19: Sie haben Terminkalender wie Top-Manager.

So wie Dagmar Neusser aus Düsseldorf. "Freitag ist der schlimmste Tag", sagt Dagmar und strahlt dabei.   Denn "schlimm" heisst lediglich ausgefüllt. Wenn freitags die Schule um halb zwei aus ist - und für Millionen von Arbeitnehmern das lange Wochenende beginnt -, geht's für Dagmar erst richtig los. Von der Schule hetzt sie zu ihrem Job als Turntrainerin, danach hat sie Italienischkurs, und dann geht's noch zur Jazztanzgruppe. Nach gut zwölf Stunden Hektik kommt sie um neun nach Hause. Dort warten noch einmal zwei Stunden Hausaufgaben auf sie.

Die Psychologin Dr. Katharina Holzheuer vom Evangelischen Beratungszentrum in München kennt solche Stundenpläne aus ihrer Praxis. "Neben der Schule existieren eine Menge Aktivitäten, die sehr häufig leistungsorientiert absolviert werden." Nach ihrer Erfahrung wird Rumhängen als Belastung erlebt. Action ist angesagt, und dafür werden auch Unannehmnlichkeiten in Kauf genommen.

Anja Beckert aus Saarbrücken ist erst fünfzehn, doch ein Ziel hat sie schon ganz fest im Visier. "Ich will Opernsängerin werden. Es sei denn", schränkt sie ein, "meine Stimme trägt nicht." Seit die Gymnasiastin als Chorsängerin in Humperdincks "Hänsel und Gretel" auf der Bühne stand, liebt sie das Theater im allgemeinen und die Oper im besonderen.

Als Statistin am Saarländischen Staatstheater muss sie Disziplin und Pünktlichkeit beweisen. Nachmittags hat sie Probe für eine Neuinszenierung, am Abend Vorstellung. Sie hat bei rund hundert Aufführungen mitgewirkt, Proben nicht mitgerechnet.

Fühlt sie sich nicht manchmal gestresst? Sie schaut mich nach dieser Frage an, als wolle ich sie beleidigen. Stress, was ist das? Schliesslich bleibt ihr ja immer noch genügend Zeit, ihren Brieffreunden in Kanada, Schweden, Spanien, Kenia, Peru, Frankreich und der DDR (uff!) zu schreiben, Klavierstunden zu nehmen und zum Jazztanz zu gehen. Ach ja, und in einer Jury, die Stücke für ein Schülertheater-Festival aussucht, sitzt das zarte Kind auch noch.

Das einzige, was ihr in letzter Zeit auf den Magen geschlagen sei, "ist die Sache mit der Schülerzeitung an meinem Gymnasium". Weil es mit der Teamarbeit im Redaktionskollektiv nicht mehr klappte, hob Anja mit sieben Gehilfinnen eine Konkurrenzzeitung aus der Taufe. Und ganz nebenbei gehört sie auch noch zu den Besten ihrer Klasse.

Alexandra von Prittwitz, Dekorateurlehrling in München, hatte mit Schule nie viel am Hut. Doch an ehrgeizigen Plänen mangelt es auch ihr nicht. Ihr Ziel: einmal als Möbeldesignerin in New York zu leben. Sie ist selbstbewusst und optimistisch.

Nix "No future", obwohl sie wie ein Punker aussieht: Die Haare lila, grün und rosa gescheckt, Jackett und Hose sehen aus, als stammten sie aus einer DRK-Kleidersammlung. Nur ihre Manieren sind äusserst gepflegt. "Ich stehe in der U-Bahn auf und biete einer alten Dame meinen Platz an. Und ich mag es, wenn mir jemand die Tür aufhält, mir in den Mantel hilft."

Alexandra raucht nicht, trinkt am liebsten Kakao und hört mit Leidenschaft Beethoven. Nach ihrem Acht-Stunden-Tag im Kaufhaus geht sie in die Oper oder zu Vernissagen.

Ihr Motto: Man muss nicht alles studiert haben, aber man muss viel ausprobieren, mitmachen, um zu wissen, wo die eigenen Stärken liegen. So ging sie gegen ein geringes Entgelt als Au-pair-Mädchen nach England, öffnete Austern bei einem Münchner Feinkosthändler und half bei Partys, durstigen Gästen die Gläser zu füllen. "Alles, was ich mache, bringt mich meinem Ziel ein Stückchen näher", so ihre Überzeugung, "und mein Ziel bin ich selbst."

(*Bunte*, 10.9.87)

Preparation: practising conditional constructions

Diskutieren Sie, ob Sie auch so viele Freizeitbeschäftigungen haben möchten.

    BEISPIEL: Wenn Sie Zeit hätten, würden Sie auch in die Oper gehen?

Bilden Sie weitere Fragen nach diesem Muster:

1. eine gute Stimme haben - Opernsängerin werden
2. nur vormittags Schule haben - nachmittags Italienischkurs machen
3. kein Geld haben - durstigen Gästen Gläser füllen
4. Platz in der U-Bahn - älterer Dame anbieten
5. Zeit haben - Beethoven hören

A classroom survey

Umfrage in der Klasse: Was machst du in der Freizeit?

Examples 21 & 22 introduced

Example 21 has as its culminating activity a simulated interview with Ivan Beshoff, last survivor of the Potemkin mutiny. As with the various writing activities described above, so here the authentic text is thoroughly processed before the role play is attempted. The fact that the first three activities could equally well be used to prepare for a written task should again warn us against assuming that most learning activities are tied to one particular language skill. Our last illustration in this chapter, Example 22, underlines this point: the brief authentic text provides the stimulus and content for a survey of how learners spend their free time; the survey is conducted orally in Spanish; and the results of the survey are then used to rewrite the Spanish text. In this instance the blending of language skills is accompanied by a merging of the two orders of authenticity to give what is potentially a deeply satisfying chain of activities.

EXAMPLE 21

Le dernier survivant du cuirassé «Potemkine» est mort en Irlande

Le dernier survivant connu de la mutinerie du cuirassé *Potemkine*, M. Ivan Beshoff, est décédé dimanche 25 octobre, à son domicile de Dublin.

M. Beshoff était ingénieur-mécanicien à bord du *Potemkine*, cuirassé de la flotte impériale russe de la mer Noire, lorsque l'équipage se révolta, le 14 juin 1905, après l'exécution d'un matelot par un officier.

L'armada russe avait alors reçu l'ordre d'attaquer le *Potemkine* et de mater la rébellion, mais les équipages des autres bateaux avaient refusé de tirer sur leurs camarades.

Dans un entretien récent, Ivan Beshoff, membre à l'époque du Parti social-démocrate russe, expliquait qu'il s'était alors enfui clandestinement en Angleterre, où il avait rencontré Lénine. Puis, avec d'autres mutins, il avait gagné l'Amérique du Sud avant de s'établir définitivement en 1913 en Irlande, où il a d'abord travaillé pour une société pétrolière soviétique. Il y a été arrêté deux fois, accusé d'espionnage au profit de l'Union soviétique. Après la seconde guerre mondiale, il avait ouvert un florissant restaurant de *«fish and chips»* (poissons et frites) à Dublin.

(*Le Monde*, 29.10.87)

Explain selected words contained in the authentic text

1. Expliquez les mots suivants avant de lire l'article: Potemkine; Lénine; mer Noire; flotte impériale; mutinerie; cuirassée; matelot; armada. Vous pouvez, si nécessaire, utiliser un dictionnaire.

Read the text and replace the words with your definitions

2. Lisez l'article. Maintenant remplacez dans l'article (oralement ou par écrit) les mots de la liste précédente par les définitions que vous avez trouvées.

Consider how the meaning of the text has been changed

3. Le sens du texte est-il le même? Si ce n'est pas le cas, demandez au prof. de vous aider à trouver des définitions plus précises.

Group work/ role play: an interview based on the authentic text

4. Divisez la classe en groupes de deux. A l'aide du plan ci-dessous, imaginez un interview de M. Ivan Beshoff.
   (a) Journaliste: demande à M. Beshoff de se présenter (âge, origine, etc. ...)
   (b) M. Beshoff: réponse
   (c) Journaliste: demande à M. Beshoff où il se trouvait en 1905 et ce qu'il faisait

(d)   M. Beshoff: réponse

EXAMPLE 22

¿Y tú qué haces?
Según las últimas encuestas, los jóvenes de los Pirineos hacia abajo escogen para su tiempo libre estas alternativas: salir con los amigos (calle, bares ...), 79%; ver TV o video, 63%; esuchar música, 60%; salir de copas, 53%; lectura, 42%; cine, 34%; radio, 30%; deporte, 28%; excursiones camprestres, 22%; espectáculos deportivos, 20%; salir con el novio/a, 19%; tocar un instrumento musical, 12%; actividades políticas, 9%; asociaciones recreativas, 7%; teatro, 7%; otras, 5%. «Dime qué haces cuando no haces nada y te diré quién eres».

(em, 11/87)

Conduct a classroom survey in Spanish and use the results to rewrite the authentic text

Conduct a survey in Spanish among your classmates to see how they spend their leisure time. Ask questions like:

¿Cuántas veces por semana sales con tus amigos?
¿Practicas algún deporte?
¿Vas muy a menudo al cine?

When you have finished, rewrite the Spanish article, replacing the results of the original survey with your own results.

Suggestions for further reading

Two books by H. G. Widdowson contain a wealth of ideas that can be applied to authentic texts: *Teaching Language as Communication* (already mentioned at the end of Chapter 2) and *Stylistics and the Teaching of Literature* (London: Longman; 1975). The communicative exercise typology developed by German applied linguists and language teachers at the end of the 1970s likewise contains many ideas that can readily be adapted to authentic texts. It has been published in several forms, including *Übungstypologie zum kommunikativen Deutschunterricht*, by G. Neuner, M. Krüger and U. Grewer (Langenscheidt: Munich; 1981) and *The Communicative Teaching of English*, edited by C. N. Candlin (London: Longman; 1981). Another rich source of material on classroom activities relevant to work with authentic texts is *Communication in the Modern Languages Classroom*, by J. Sheils (Strasbourg: Council of Europe; 1988).

Three CLCS Occasional Papers (published by the Centre for Language and Communication Studies, Trinity College, Dublin) discuss issues closely related to the central concerns of this chapter: No.18 - *Learning a foreign language through the media*, by S. Devitt; No.20 - *Authentic materials and the role of fixed support in language teaching: towards a manual for language learners*, by D. Little and D. Singleton; and No.21 - *Classroom discourse: its nature and its potential for language learning*, by S. Devitt.

Chapter 4

Using authentic texts to develop learners' conscious control of the target language

Pedagogical procedures and largely unconscious acquisition processes

Much of our argument so far has associated pedagogical procedures with what we know about largely unconscious language acquisition processes; the basis of the argument being that the essentially artificial process of language teaching is most likely to succeed to the extent that it manages to activate natural processes of language acquisition. At the same time, many of the activities illustrated in Chapter 3, especially in sections 3 and 4, are underpinned by analytical procedures that depend on a developing awareness of how language works as a formal system. For example, some of the more elaborate exercise chains begin with a preparatory activity that focuses on the organization of vocabulary; while activities that require learners to edit or rewrite text inevitably bring grammar into the foreground. There are two reasons why these analytical procedures are an essential part of language learning. First, the demands and constraints that a formal educational context imposes will always make it necessary to support unconscious processes of acquisition with a deliberate effort of conscious and analytical learning. Secondly, all linguistic communication that requires planning, monitoring and editing is possible only to the extent that we have developed a capacity for reflection and analysis.

Many of the activities illustrated in Chapter 3 underpinned by analytical procedures

Why analytical procedures are an essential part of language learning

These considerations are fundamental to this chapter, which focuses on how we should set about developing the different kinds of conscious knowledge that are essential to language competence. We have argued in the preceding chapters that successful language development is most likely to occur in the classroom context when learners are engaged in the processing of authentic texts, and that the

Authentic texts as promoters of language learning

71

more the texts are related to the learners' personal concerns and interests the deeper and more rapid the processing will be. The availability of a regular supply of authentic texts catering for a wide range of learner interests is now no longer a problem thanks to Authentik.

In this chapter we look in more detail at what is involved in processing texts. We begin by describing the processes of reading and listening and analysing the different kinds of knowledge on which they depend, and we then briefly relate the same kinds of knowledge to the process of writing. We go on to argue that words constitute the basic level of linguistic knowledge required for any of these processes, and we consider what is meant by knowing words, how they are stored and accessed, and how they are best learned. We then look briefly at authentic texts as sources of input for learning vocabulary and syntax. Next we present a model for developing each level of knowledge, both linguistic and non-linguistic, through authentic texts; and we argue that examination tasks are best prepared for through such a developmental model. Then we use worked examples in French, German and Spanish to illustrate how the different kinds of knowledge required for language comprehension and production may be developed. We end the chapter with some general reflections that also serve as a conclusion to the book as a whole.

4.1 The processes of reading, listening and writing

Research has shown that reading is not simply a matter of deciphering a set of printed symbols. Rather, it involves an interaction between the information contained in those symbols and the reader's prior knowledge. In other words, it is not simply a question of working from the bottom up, from the symbols to their meaning and message; we simultaneously work from the top down, using what we already know to interpret what we see in front of us. A particular act of reading may confirm our prior knowledge, expand it, or modify it in some way, allowing new elements to be integrated.

The kinds of knowledge that readers bring to the task of reading are the same as those they bring to the task of language learning - world knowledge, discourse knowledge, and linguistic knowledge (since "naturalistic" language learning takes places *via* communication, it is hardly surprising that language acquisition and language processing should be so closely related). It seems that our world knowledge is organized into a mass of interrelated networks of what some theorists call "schemata". To take a simple example, our knowledge of kidnaps might have a "schema" of the type illustrated in Figure 1.

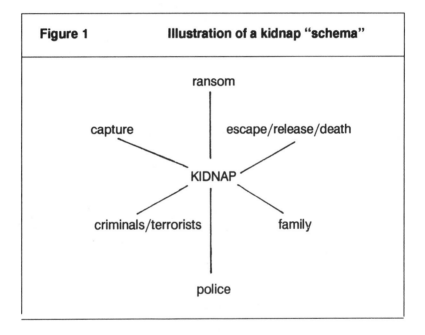

Figure 1   Illustration of a kidnap "schema"

A specific kidnap would have in addition certain details of time, place, transport, and so on. We use general "schemata" for interpreting texts dealing with incidents with which we are not familiar, and more elaborate "schemata" when we are already familiar with the incident in question. "Schemata" are often further elaborated into "scripts", corresponding to the way we would expect events to happen or to be written about. A general kidnap "script" might run as follows:

businessman/woman kidnapped in <place>
                           at <time>
kidnappers take him/her in car <type>
family receives ransom note for <amount of money>
family approaches police
either: criminals kill businessman/woman
or: businessman/woman is freed or escapes

Prior knowledge
also important
in process of
listening

Listening, whether reciprocal (e.g. when one is taking part in a conversation) or non-reciprocal (e.g. when one is listening to a radio broadcast or lecture), is also a very active process involving interpretation of the incoming sounds in terms of what we already know. "Schemata" and "scripts" play much the same role in listening as they do in reading.

Interaction
of linguistic
knowledge with
knowledge of
the topic

Figure 2
interpreted

We have claimed that the processing of authentic texts in a foreign language through reading and listening provides the input that is essential for language development. Figure 2 illustrates a range of possible situations in which knowledge of the language (vertical axis) interacts with knowledge of the topic (horizontal axis). We can plot nine different points, labelled from A to I, representing nine possible combinations of the two types of knowledge. A and I are both extreme cases. A is the person who knows the language and already knows the content of what he is reading; no new information is communicated relative to language or content. I is at the other extreme; he knows nothing either of the content or of the language, so that no information can be communicated. The other seven points represent the normal range of readers. B and C know the language fully but the content not at all or only partially; in other words, they are native speakers reading about a more or less unfamiliar topic. D and G know the language not at all or only partially but are totally familiar with the topic; they might be language learners reading a target language text about something already known to them - perhaps a well-known fairy tale or a recent news item. There is no significant new information at the level of content, but using established "schemata" and "scripts" they can learn a lot about the target language. H, E and F have levels of content and linguistic knowledge ranging from some to none. They might be language learners reading about old news items that they have forgotten or the details of which are incomplete in their memory; or perhaps about an incident which is totally unknown to them but which matches some element in their experience.

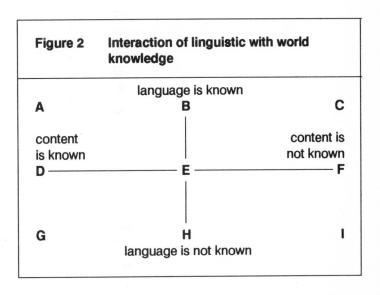

Figure 2 Interaction of linguistic with world knowledge

Language learners in relation to Figure 2

Most language learners coping with authentic texts belong somewhere in the lower half of Figure 2 - their precise point on the horizontal axis will depend on how familiar they are with the topic of what they are reading or listening to. Obviously, the more they know about the topic, the more processing "space" is available for the language. It will often be necessary for them to create this space by constructing "schemata" and "scripts" in advance of reading or listening. Furthermore, since vocabulary knowledge has been found to be the single most important factor in determining reading ability in first and second languages, it may be important to do preparatory work with words. Working with the key words of a text *in the target language* in order to create the necessary "schemata" and "scripts" combines these two steps in an elegant and highly efficient way (cf. the examples in 3.3 and 3.4).

Knowledge of topic creates processing "space" for language

Equally, it may be necessary to provide simplified versions of a text in order to facilitate language processing. The examples in Chapter 3 and later in this chapter give ample

Using simplified texts to facilitate language-processing

illustration of how this might be done in a way that involves the learner actively. Ideally, the materials with which learners are provided will include spoken as well as written manifestations of words in isolation and in context. This can be an especially important aspect of preparation for listening, since authentic oral texts are often spoken at a speed that allows little time for processing.

The desirability of providing spoken as well as written forms of words

We now turn briefly to writing, which might be described as the process of putting ideas together in a meaningful way for a reader or readers. In writing, as in reading and listening, we use "schemata" and "scripts" to organize our ideas; and once again our knowledge of vocabulary is fundamental. After all, fluency in writing depends on our knowing words appropriate to the expression of what we want to say and knowing how those words behave structurally, in relation to one another.

"Schemata" and "scripts" in writing

In Chapter 3 we included a number of examples that required learners to organize words and phrases into a telegraphic text as the first step towards understanding the authentic text from which those words and phrases had been derived. We emphasized that the value of such a text must in the first instance be measured by the extent to which it aids the process of comprehension. But a strong case can be made for always beginning the process of writing by producing a telegraphic text. An approach that begins by trying to construct the text correct sentence by correct sentence often fails to produce overall coherence; whereas the examples of learners' texts that we quoted in Chapter 3 (see pp.54f. above) show how a telegraphic text can possess overall coherence while being deficient in cohesion at the level of the individual sentence.

Telegraphic texts as an aid to writing

4.2 Vocabulary

Since vocabulary is central to reading, listening and writing, it is important to consider how it is learned, what is involved in "knowing" a word, how words are stored in long-term memory, and how they are accessed. The first thing to note about vocabulary is that it exists on a continuum that

Vocabulary central to reading, listening and writing

runs from zero knowledge to total mastery. Table 1 illustrates some of the principal points on the continuum. In
order to be able to use words in speech or writing the learner
needs to know what semantic networks they belong to, how
they behave syntactically, and what limitations constrain
their use. Of course, not all words are learned for productive
use, even in our first language. Moreover, we should not
think of our vocabulary store as being static. At any particular stage we will have words at all points along the continuum we have schematized in Table 1.

Table 1	Principal points on the vocabulary continuum
Levels	**What the learner can do in relation to particular word**
Established	able to give full meaning
	able to give part of correct meaning
	able to give general sense
	recognizes it out of context
Acquainted	able to recognize all forms in context
	able to recognize principal forms in context
	able to guess meaning from context but forgets quickly
Unknown	has seen/heard the word but does not know what it means
	has never seen/heard the word before

How we store
words in long-
term memory

Researchers are generally agreed that words are stored
in our long-term memory in networks of overlapping semantic fields (e.g. *dog, cat, cow, chicken, turkey*), but also, within

particular syntactic category, according to sound (e.g. the nouns *cat*, *hat*, *mat*, etc.). It seems that we store the sound of a word in its citation form (what we look up in the dictionary). Both meaning and sound are used for retrieving words from memory - the "tip-of-the-tongue" phenomenon and malapropisms give ample evidence of this. Obviously, knowing a word involves the ability not only to recognize it in isolation but to be able to pick it out in a stream of speech.

Two views of how vocabulary is learned

How is vocabulary learned? As far as first languages are concerned, there are two schools of thought. One argues that words must be learned naturally in context, while the other advocates formal vocabulary teaching, especially for weaker learners. The research evidence supports both groups.

Learning by meeting words in context

On the one hand, vocabulary growth occurs *via* reading, but in very small increments; words move slowly along the continuum we have described above. However, the more the learner reads, the quicker this process becomes and the greater the number of words on the continuum.

Teaching vocabulary formally

On the other hand, formal vocabulary teaching has also been shown to be very effective, especially for moving certain key words more rapidly along the continuum. In particular it has been found that vocabulary is learned more rapidly when it is taught in semantic fields related to the kind of texts that learners need to be able to read. Accordingly, the most efficient way of developing the vocabulary store would appear to be one that combines both approaches. Ideally,

Combining both modes of vocabulary learning

explicit teaching of a word should combine the citation form *spoken* so as to aid storage in long-term memory, with examples of the word in use so as to aid recognition and begin to develop a sense of how it behaves syntactically.

The fact that reading and listening depend crucially on vocabulary does not mean that second language learners are obliged to wait until substantial vocabulary growth has taken place before they attempt to read or listen to authentic materials in their target language. On the contrary, the

Reading and listening can support vocabulary development

development of vocabulary in a second language can be supported by reading and listening in much the same way as happens in first languages.

It is now possible to present a schematic overview of our

TABLE 2

COMPONENTS OF READING, LISTENING AND WRITING PROCESSES

Result	Linguistic knowledge	Other knowledge
Writing Production of a grammaticalized text		
	2b Syntax beyond the sentence (e.g. discourse markers, use of pro-forms, etc.)	
	2a Morpho-syntax of basic sentence (e.g. word order, morphology etc.)	
Reading & listening Finding the message of a text		
Writing Transmitting a message through a text in telegraphic form but with correct discourse structure		**0b** Knowledge of discourse
	1 Vocabulary stores (including information about words, their networks) [Linguistic data bases]	**0a** General knowledge frameworks (world knowledge, knowledge of the topic)

model of reading, listening and writing. In Table 2 world knowledge and discourse knowledge, labelled 0a and 0b respectively, are given on the right hand side. The vocabulary store, which we take to be the basic level of linguistic knowledge, we have labelled 1. With this basic level of linguistic knowledge we can already create discourse, as we showed in Chapter 3 with two texts produced by learners of French (see p.55 above). In each case the learners either already possessed the components of what happened or else created them from their world knowledge (0a); they then matched the vocabulary they already possessed or had been given (1) to the components of the event; and they used their knowledge of discourse structure (0b) to create their own texts, to transmit a message.

Knowledge of morpho-syntax at sentence level and knowledge of syntax beyond sentence level are labelled 2a and 2b respectively. Much of the "naturalistic" language acquisition process involves the gradual grammaticalization of basic discourse, that is, learning how to mark the various elements of discourse according to the grammatical conventions of the language in question. The two learner texts cited in Chapter 3 provide examples of different stages in this process: the boy in his first year of learning French did not have the linguistic ability to go beyond the level of basic discourse, whereas the four girls in their second year of learning showed some progress in the development of their morpho-syntactic knowledge. Accurate written production requires detailed knowledge of this type. In comprehension this extra level of knowledge may be less important, providing us with further information to help us find the message of the text, but mainly in the form of checks. But both production and comprehension involve the same components and move in the same direction.

We can now list what needs to be done to develop each component of the reading, listening and writing model (numbers are those given to the different components in Table 2):

Marginal notes:

Table 2 interpreted

Creating discourse with basic level of linguistic knowledge

Knowledge of morpho-syntax at sentence level and knowledge of syntax beyond sentence level

The learner texts cited in Chapter 3 and the development of syntactic knowledge

Summary of
what is needed
to develop each
component of
the reading,
listening and
writing model

Comprehension

0a   Develop the skill of using world knowledge ("schemata").
Add relevant cultural knowledge for the target language to existing world knowledge.

0b   Develop the skill of using knowledge of discourse structure ("scripts").
Add relevant information about specific target language discourse structures.

1   Build up vocabulary store, especially in ranges specified by the syllabus.
Build up information about the networks of associations between words and about what words combine with one another.

0a & 1   Develop the skill of relating vocabulary to world knowledge to create meaningful clusters.
Develop the skill of organizing the elements of these clusters to get to the message of the text.

2a & 2b   Develop the skill of using morpho-syntax and discourse markers to check the message.

Production

0a   Develop world knowledge in relevant domains.

0b   Develop the knowledge of target language discourse structures where relevant, e.g., for letters, both formal and informal, for reports, descriptions, narrative, etc.

1   Build up vocabulary store, especially in ranges specified by the syllabus. Build up information about the networks of associations between words and about what words combine with one another.

0a & 1   Develop the skill of relating vocabulary to world knowledge to create meaningful clusters.

0a, 0b & 1   Develop the skill of organizing the elements of these clusters to create meaningful text.

2a   Develop morpho-syntactic knowledge at simple sentence level in order to edit texts.

2b   Develop knowledge of syntax beyond the

simple sentence and of the relevant discourse conventions and markers.

4.3 Examinations

Let us turn briefly to examination tasks and their relation to the model we have just presented. We have been considering the use of authentic texts from a language learning perspective, as sources of linguistic input, and have outlined ways in which learners can be helped to in process this input so as to develop vocabulary, syntax and discourse.

Examinations: a "language learned" perspective

Examinations, on the other hand, take a "language learned" perspective. They try to determine how well and accurately candidates can understand the content of an authentic text or themselves express content through the target language. The testing of comprehension is typically carried out at lower levels by questions about the factual content of simple texts, while writing is likely to involve the production of a fairly straightforward text. At more advanced levels both the texts and the tasks to be performed become more complex, often involving some combination of the different skills of listening, reading, speaking and writing. However, apart from cloze tests and translation into the target language (see sections 4.4 and 4.5 below), the kinds of tasks required even at higher levels are made up of the components we have given above for listening, reading and writing.

Using exam questions to prepare learners for exams

Many teachers feel that the best way of preparing their learners for examinations is to give them plenty of practice in just those tasks which the examinations require. We suggest, however, that by developing the components of the skills we have indicated, teachers can prepare them not only for examinations but also for using the target language as a medium of communication in real life.

An alternative approach

Focussing on examination skills is restricting and ultimately sterile; developing the components of these skills is much more interesting and productive.

Table 3 and the appendix

Table 3 shows how typical examination tasks can be related to the model of listening, reading and writing we have presented (the appendix provides an analysis of the text types and tasks used in the various public examinations for which learners are prepared in the United Kingdom).

82

TABLE 3

**COMPONENTS OF READING, LISTENING AND WRITING PROCESSES
RELATED TO TYPICAL EXAMINATION TASKS**

CL	Cloze tests
Com	Comprehension of text
L	Letter writing
R	Report, summary or message writing, based on notes or text
O	Expressing opinions, with or without guidelines
N	Narrative
T1	Translation from target language
T2	Translation into target language

Exam tasks

Components	CL	Com	L	R,O,N,	T1	T2
2b Syntax beyond the sentence	Develop	Use as check	Develop	Develop	Use as check	Develop
2a Syntax of simple sentence	Develop	Use as check	Develop	Develop	Use as check	Develop
1 Vocab. stores	Develop	Develop	Develop	Develop	Develop	Develop
0b Knowledge of discourse structures	Use	Use	Develop	Use or given	Use and develop	Use and develop
0a Knowledge of world, topic	Use	Use	Use	Given	Use	Use
Skill of linking 0a and 1	Develop	Develop	Develop			

We treat cloze tests separately for two reasons. First, it is not always clear what exactly the cloze tests included in public examinations are intended to test. Secondly, we take the view that cloze technique is not just a testing mechanism; it can also be used constructively within the model we have presented as a way of developing vocabulary, morpho-syntax and discourse.

4.4 Cloze technique as a way of coming to grips with words in context

Definition of cloze technique

In its classic form cloze technique involves deleting words from a text and requiring the learner to insert an appropriate word in each gap. Some cloze exercises require only linguistic knowledge; in others world and discourse knowledge also have a role to play, since some gaps can be filled only if we have an idea of what the text is about. But every cloze exercise makes us focus on words in context.

Using cloze exercises to develop linguistic skills

What skills can be developed with the help of cloze exercises? At single word level learners need vocabulary; this may be specifically related to the topic of the text - for example, *cinema, film, screen, box-office,* - or may be general. At sentence level they need to know what changes to make to the basic word in order for it to be morphologically and syntactically acceptable in the position in which it occurs. This demands a knowledge both of the appropriate forms and of their corresponding uses. Learners also need to know how the different parts of a text relate to one another. For example, some of the deleted words may be explicit dis-course markers, like *however* and *therefore*; others, like pronouns, may contribute to the cohesion of the text in less obvious ways. In any case, most missing elements contribute to the coherence of a text in important ways and will therefore have to relate meaningfully to other elements in the text.

An example should help to illustrate the different skills required. Let us take a well-known fable of Aesop, first of all in telegraphic form:

Cloze exercise
based on
telegraphic
version of Aesop
fable

Crow find cheese.
Crow eat cheese.
Fox see crow.
Fox praise (1) _____ of crow.
Crow sing.
Crow (2) ____ cheese.
Fox pick up cheese.
Fox run away.

Issues raised by
this exercise

To do this cloze exercise learners must understand the text, decide on the meaning and function of the missing words (noun, belonging to crow, related to *sing*, direct object of *praise*; verb, let fall), and retrieve the appropriate words *voice* and *drop* from their active vocabulary. In terms of Table 2, the only components required are 0a (world knowledge) and 1 (vocabulary).

In a more elaborated form of the text this knowledge will still be required; in addition, however, learners will have to be able to select the appropriate form of the words chosen. Here is a cloze exercise based on one of a set of variations on the theme by James Thurber:

Cloze exercise
based on
elaborated
version of
Aesop fable

A fox, attracted by the scent of something, followed his nose to a tree in which (1) _____ a crow with a piece of cheese in his beak. "Oh, cheese," said the fox (2)_____. "That's for mice."

The crow removed the cheese with his talons and said, "You always hate the thing you cannot have, as, for instance, grapes."

"Grapes are for the birds," said the fox haughtily. "I am an epicure, a gourmet, and a gastronome."

The embarrassed crow, ashamed to be seen (3)_____ mouse food by a great specialist in the art of dining, hastily (4)_____ the cheese. The fox caught it deftly, swallowed it with relish, said "Merci," politely, and trotted away.

Different kinds
of knowledge
and different
kinds of error

In the case of the missing verbs, the learner has not only to know the correct words, but also their tense and the form in which to express that tense. If he writes *sit* for (1), he shows he has the correct meaning; *sitted* would indicate knowledge of the correct tense; while *sat* would indicate knowledge of meaning, tense and form. Either of the two "wrong" options does, therefore, show a certain level of linguistic competence which should be recognized. What of the option *eat* for *eating* in (3), or *droped* instead of *dropped* in (4)? And what about other options for *scornfully* in (2)? Relating this to Table 2 above, we can see that we again require components 0a and 1, but also 2a (morpho-syntactic knowledge at sentence level) and at least some 2b (syntax beyond the sentence) since the choice of tense depends on other elements in the text.

Definite and indefinite articles focus on syntax above sentence level

If we used the Thurber text to create a cloze exercise in which we deleted *a* before the first occurrence of *crow* in the first paragraph, *the* before the second occurrence of *fox* in the same paragraph, and *an* before *epicure* in the third paragraph, leaving a space also before *grapes* in the same paragraph, we would be getting learners to focus on a small closed set of words, the choice of which is almost totally dependent on the position within the discourse of the noun in question. The knowledge required for this task would be mostly 2b (syntax beyond sentence level), with some knowledge of syntax at sentence level if there were a question of grammatical agreement between article and noun. On the

Prepositions focus on morpho-syntax

other hand, if the words omitted were prepositions, for example, *by*, *to* or *in* in the first paragraph, very little would be required apart from some minimal morpho-syntactic knowledge (2a).

4.5 Translation into the target language

Translation a special case

Translation into the target language is a special case and a difficult exercise at any stage of language development. We pointed out in Table 3 that the components that need to be developed for translation are vocabulary and syntax at and above sentence level. How might translation as an activity be associated with the exercises we have presented in this and the previous chapter?

Problems created by word-for-word translation

Perhaps the single most common fault among learners is word-for-word translation. This creates havoc with both sentence and discourse structure. In order to get learners to translate ideas and not words and to produce something

86

which reads reasonably well, whether in English or their target language, it is possible to prepare the ground by using the types of exercise we have outlined above. Learners might, for example, be asked to compose on the basis of key words first rather than translate. This would guarantee a coherent text, which might then be gradually adapted to match what has to be translated. Even translating telegraphic target-language texts into corresponding telegraphic English can have its value, sensitizing learners to the importance of coherence in discourse and at the same time serving as the first draft of a translation of the original passage.

Using key words and telegraphic texts to prepare a translation

4.6 Developing the different components and skills: three examples

(i) The three texts

Three texts chosen to illustrate practical techniques

As we explained at the beginning of this chapter, we have chosen three texts, one in French, one in German and one in Spanish, as the basis for illustrating the practical techniques we propose for developing the different kinds of knowledge required by the reading, and writing skills. Two of the texts are narratives, the third is a combination of narrative, profile and evaluation. The techniques we suggest here are, we believe, applicable to a wide range of text types.

The French example introduced

The French example is taken from an article entitled "Victime de son courage", which appeared in *Le Parisien* of 5 October 1987 and was published in the November 1987 issue of *Authentik en Français*. It deals with a man who helped save 27 children from a fire in Besançon and as a result developed a respiratory condition which caused him to lose his job; he was then threatened with eviction:

VICTIME DE SON COURAGE

En avril 1985, alors qu'un incendie ravageait son immeuble, Camille Tournier avait arraché vingt-sept adolescents du brasier. Gravement intoxiqué par la fumée il avait perdu son emploi. Aujourd'hui, alors qu'il est privé de ressources, et dans l'attente d'une opération, le gérant de son immeuble veut le faire expulser. Mais les locataires, reconnaissants, prennent sa défense.

... Ce jour-là, Camille Tournier, quarante et un ans, se précipite dans les couloirs de son bâtiment ravagé par un incendie. L'épaisse fumée produite par la combustion des matières isolantes a envahi la cage d'escalier où jouent habituellement les gamins.

Avec deux autres habitants de l'immeuble, Camille leur fraie un passage vers une trappe de secours: elle est condamnée par une chaîne! Il ne se désespère pas et, suivi par la petite troupe, il réussit enfin à pénétrer dans un appartement d'où les pompiers, avec une grande échelle, évacueront les vingt-sept enfants.

Cet acte de bravoure, Camille va le payer cher. Gravement intoxiqué par la fumée, touché au poumon, le coeur faiblissant, il doit être hospitalisé dans un état désespéré. La maladie ne l'emportera pas mais Camille Tournier devra pourtant ensuite abandonner son travail de surveillant de magasin. Ses absences répétées, dues à des malaises, ont lassé son employeur. Et Camille, qui a un enfant à charge, s'est bien vite retrouvé sans ressources...

The German example introduced The German text is an extract from the article about twins, "Zwei Leben - ein Schicksal", originally published in *Quick* Nr. 53/87 and already reprinted in Chapter 3. The article appeared in the February 1988 edition of *Authentik auf Deutsch*:

... Die beiden wurden am 7. Juli 1939 als Gerda und Erika Wegener in Berlin-Karlshorst (heute DDR-Gebiet) geboren. Während der Bombennächte 1943 kam Gerda - damals vier Jahre alt - mit Lungenentzündung ins Krankenhaus. Wegen der Luftangriffe wurde sie eines Nachts Hals über Kopf mit allen anderen Patienten nach Leipzig evakuiert.

Beim Transport ging das Namensbändchen an ihrem Handgelenk verloren.

Aus dem Krankenhaus kam die kleine Gerda in ein Leipziger Waisenhaus, später zu einer Pflegefamilie. 1978 zog sie nach Augsburg.

Ihre Zwillingsschwester Erika war mit den Eltern in Berlin geblieben. Verzweifelt suchten die Eltern jahrelang mit Hilfe des Roten Kreuzes, den Aufenthaltsort ihrer verschollenen Tochter Gerda zu finden. Ergebnislos.

The Spanish text was given as a translation test on the 1987 Spanish Higher Level paper in the Irish Leaving Certificate Examination. We do not know where it comes from.

El 7 de junio de 1926, un anciano despistado, modestamente vestido y sin documentación alguna, es atropellado por un tranvía junto a la Plaza de Cataluña en Barcelona. Se le conduce a un hospital, donde nadie le conoce, ni consiguen saber quién es. Dos días después, poco antes de morir, por fin logran identificarlo: es ni más ni menos que Antoni Gaudí, el original arquitecto que había revolucionado artísticamente a la sociedad catalana.

Es el último cuarto del siglo XIX, cuando el joven Gaudí, originario de Reus (Gerona), procedente de una familia humilde de caldereros y que había sacado notas bastante mediocres en su carrera de arquitectura, comienza a dar sorpresas a sus conciudadanos.

Son los años dorados. Barcelona en aquella época es el centro de todo: los artistas proliferan y encuentran en esta ciudad su caldo de cultivo. Cataluña se industrializa, las ideas liberales y burguesas están en todo su pensamiento; y en la búsqueda del resurgir de la cultura catalana, aparecen movimientos como Renaixença, en donde Gaudí ocupa un lugar destacado.

El específico estilo de Gaudí es prácticamente irrepetible. Él no conoció el Modernismo, el Expresionismo ni el Superrealismo, pero los miembros de estos movimientos bien que le debieron conocer a él, ya que en determinada medida fue un poco su precursor.

(ii) Vocabulary building

It should be obvious from our discussion of the processes of reading and writing in 4.1 that vocabulary is the component that needs to be developed across the board.

How should learners go about doing this? As we have explained, research findings suggest that they should store vocabulary in semantic fields rather than in random lists because this corresponds more closely with the memory's natural storage mechanism. An A3 scrap-book or art-pad is eminently suitable for this purpose, especially when Post-its are used for each new item. (Post-its are small adhesive labels that can be attached to and removed from any surface as often as one wishes; they are particularly valuable for language exercises which involve moving linguistic elements around.)

A basic vocabulary store might be built up as in Figure 3. However, in order to work with the vocabulary of a particular text like the Thurber example quoted above we need to connect a number of semantic fields. A useful basic structure is one which interlinks sets of words for the key areas PEOPLE, PLACE, TIME, EVENT. For the Thurber text this yields the vocabulary clusters shown in Figure 4; clearly some words belong to more than one set or field. (Here and in all succeeding figures we have adopted the convention of giving nouns in lower case, verbs in capitals, and adjectives and adverbs in italics.) We have stressed the need to develop learners' knowledge of the semantic networks to which words belong and their sense of what words can combine with what other words. Tables 4 and 5 show how this might be done for the Thurber text.

Figures 5-9 and Tables 6-12 show the application of these techniques to our French, German and Spanish texts. We have bypassed the basic vocabulary store, since it would be too cumbersome here to attempt to cover all the relevant semantic fields. But for each text we show the process of clustering the vocabulary into meaningful sets and suggest how learners' knowledge of relevant semantic fields and possible collocations might be developed further. Each of the word clusters and grids can be taught, explored and tested by a variant of cloze technique. For example, after a cluster has been created, the teacher can cover over one of the elements and the learners have to use the skills required for cloze to work out what the missing element is.

In the case of the Spanish text, we have used two clusters, one for each section of the text; for the French text we have simply divided the cluster into sections to illustrate the different stages of the narrative. Had we taken the full German text (as given in Chapter 3, pp.63f. above) we might have used either separate clusters or one cluster divided.

Interlinking semantic fields

Developing learners' knowledge of semantic networks

Applying our techniques to the sample texts

Word clusters, grids and cloze technique

The word clusters derived from the sample texts

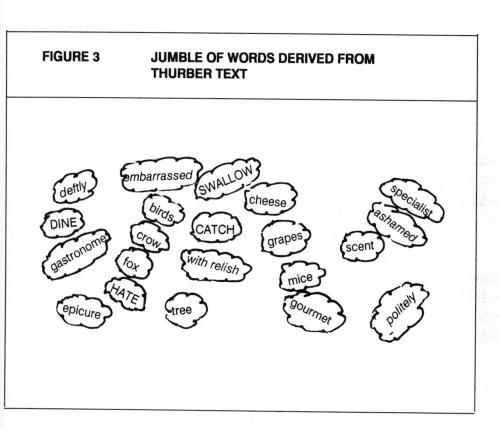

FIGURE 3   **JUMBLE OF WORDS DERIVED FROM THURBER TEXT**

91

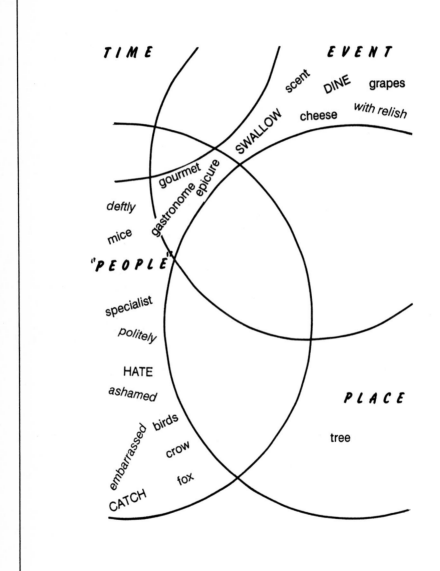

FIGURE 4   **WORDS DERIVED FROM THURBER TEXT ARRANGED IN CLUSTERS**

TIME

EVENT

scent   DINE   grapes

SWALLOW   cheese   with relish

gourmet   epicure

gastronome

deftly

mice

"PEOPLE"

specialist

politely

HATE

ashamed

PLACE

embarrassed   birds

crow

tree

CATCH   fox

TABLE 4 **THURBER TEXT:**
EXAMPLES OF SEMANTIC NETWORKS -
NOUNS AND ADJECTIVES

	clever	embarr-assed	ashamed	deftly	politely	with relish
fox	yes	yes	yes	yes	yes	yes
crow	yes	yes	yes	yes	yes	yes
birds	yes	yes	yes	yes	yes	yes
mice	yes	yes	yes	yes	yes	yes
tree						
cheese						yes
grapes						yes
talon						
beak						

TABLE 5 **THURBER TEXT:**
EXAMPLES OF COLLOCATION POSSIBILITIES -
NOUNS AND VERBS
(X= subject, Y = object)

	REMOVE	CATCH	HAVE	HATE	SAY	SWALLOW
fox	x	x/y	x	x/y	x	x
crow	x	x/y	x	x/y	x	x/y
birds	x	x/y	x/y	x/y	x	x/y
mice	x	x/y	x/y	x/y	x	x/y
cheese	y		y	y		y
grapes	y		y	y		y
talon	with	with	in			
beak	from	with	in			with

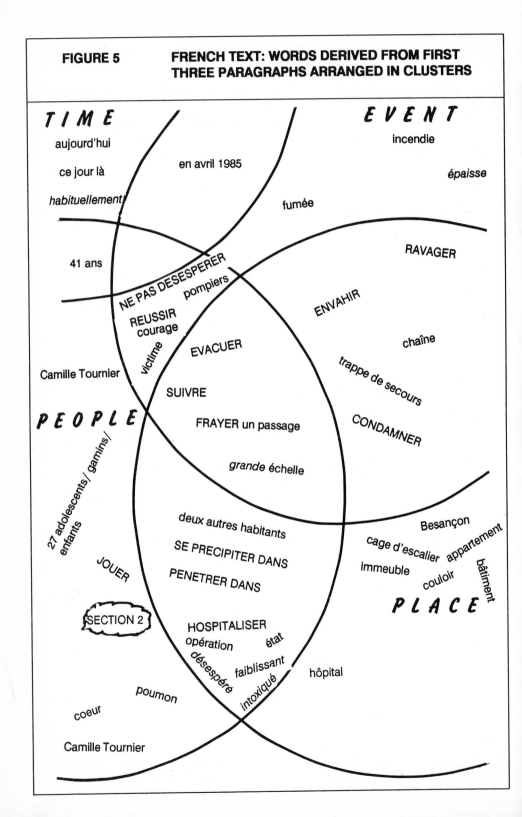

FIGURE 5   FRENCH TEXT: WORDS DERIVED FROM FIRST THREE PARAGRAPHS ARRANGED IN CLUSTERS

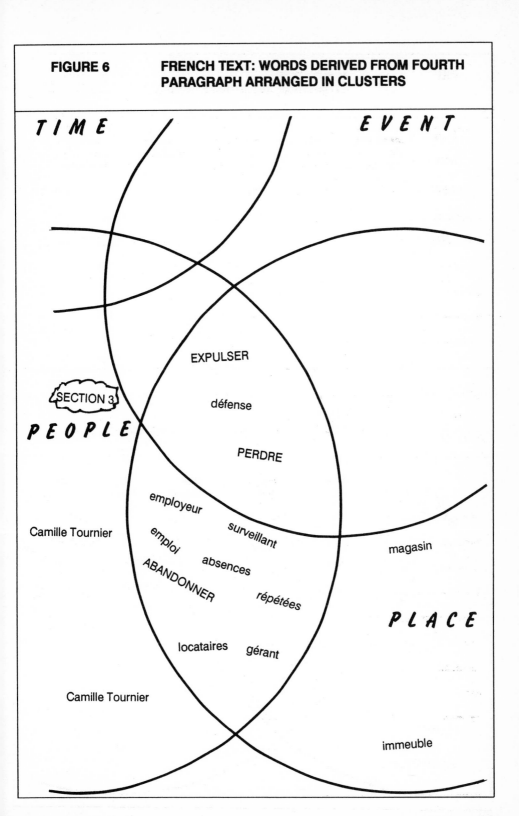

FIGURE 6   FRENCH TEXT: WORDS DERIVED FROM FOURTH PARAGRAPH ARRANGED IN CLUSTERS

95

TABLE 6   **FRENCH TEXT:**
EXAMPLES OF SEMANTIC NETWORKS

	mène une vie dangereuse	met sa vie en jeu	s'occupe de personnes	s'occupe d'affaires	s'occupe d'un immeuble
pompiers	oui	oui	oui		
gérant					oui
surveillant					oui
employeur				oui	
policier	oui		oui		
docteur			oui		
infirmière			oui		

TABLE 7   **FRENCH TEXT:**
COLLOCATION POSSIBILITIES - NOUNS AND ADJECTIVES

	grand	épais	intoxiqué	faiblissant	désespéré	répété
courage	oui					
fumée		oui				
incendie	oui					
échelle	oui					
appartement	oui					
couloir	oui					
immeuble	oui					
coeur				oui		
poumon			oui			
état					oui	
absence						oui

	payer un loyer	payer un salaire	louer un appartement	évacuer	jouer
TABLE 8		**FRENCH TEXT:**			
		EXAMPLES OF COLLOCATION POSSIBILITIES - VERBS & NOUNS			
		(X = subject, Y = object)			
gamins					X
victime				Y	
pompiers		à Y		X	
locataires	X		X/à Y		
gérant	à Y		X		
adolescent					X
surveillant		à Y			
employeur		X			
policier		à Y		X	

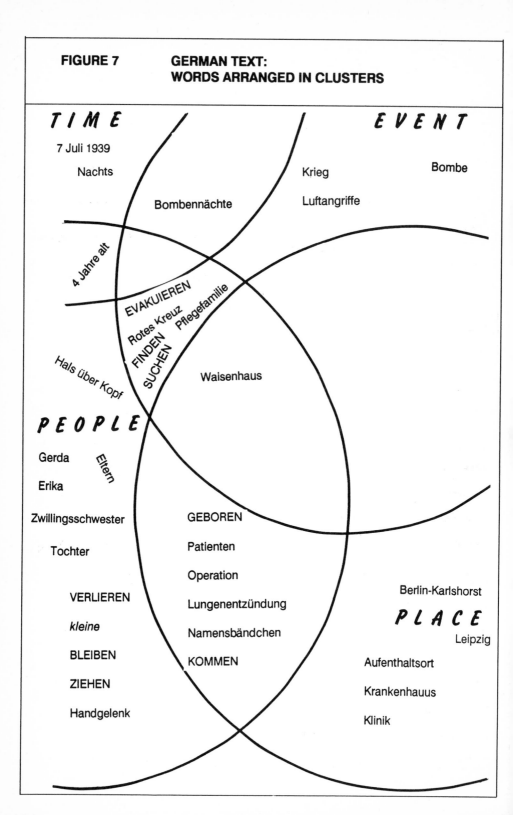

FIGURE 7   **GERMAN TEXT: WORDS ARRANGED IN CLUSTERS**

TIME

7 Juli 1939

Nachts

Bombennächte

4 Jahre alt

EVAKUIEREN

Rotes Kreuz   Pflegefamilie

FINDEN

SUCHEN

Hals über Kopf

Waisenhaus

EVENT

Krieg   Bombe

Luftangriffe

PEOPLE

Gerda   Eltern

Erika

Zwillingsschwester

Tochter

GEBOREN

Patienten

Operation

VERLIEREN   Lungenentzündung

kleine

BLEIBEN   Namensbändchen

ZIEHEN   KOMMEN

Handgelenk

Berlin-Karlshorst

PLACE

Leipzig

Aufenthaltsort

Krankenhauus

Klinik

98

TABLE 9	GERMAN TEXT: EXAMPLES OF SEMANTIC NETWORKS				
	jung	eineiig	ähnlich	mit dem Krieg assoziiert	mit dem Krankenhaus assoziiert
Eltern			ja		
Kinder	ja		ja		
Tochter	ja		ja		
Zwillinge	ja	ja	ja		
Pflege-familie				ja	
Patienten					ja
Rotes Kreuz				ja	ja

TABLE 10	GERMAN TEXT: EXAMPLES OF COLLOCATION POSSIBILITIES - VERBS & NOUNS (X = subject, Y = object)				
	schwanger sein	zur Welt bringen	geboren werden	sorgen für	evakuieren
Eltern		X		X	
Frau	X	X		X	
Kinder		Y	X	Y	Y
Zwillinge		Y	X	Y	
Patienten				Y	Y
Pflegefamilie				X	
Rotes Kreuz				X	X

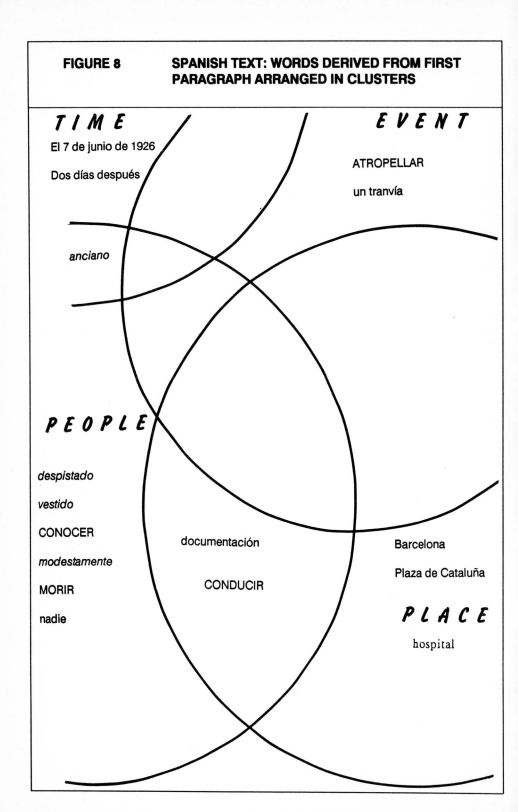

FIGURE 8   SPANISH TEXT: WORDS DERIVED FROM FIRST PARAGRAPH ARRANGED IN CLUSTERS

TIME

El 7 de junio de 1926

Dos días después

anciano

EVENT

ATROPELLAR

un tranvía

PEOPLE

despistado

vestido

CONOCER

modestamente

MORIR

nadie

documentación

CONDUCIR

Barcelona

Plaza de Cataluña

PLACE

hospital

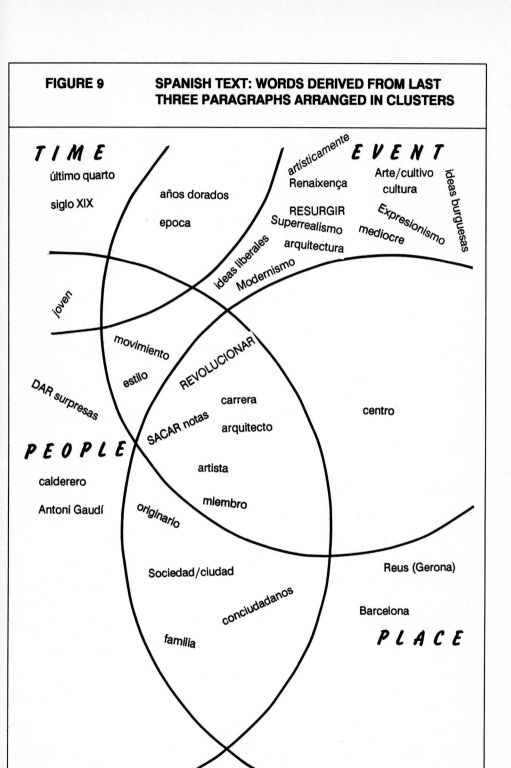

FIGURE 9   **SPANISH TEXT: WORDS DERIVED FROM LAST THREE PARAGRAPHS ARRANGED IN CLUSTERS**

TIME

último quarto

siglo XIX

años dorados

epoca

artísticamente

Renaixença

EVENT

Arte/cultivo

cultura

ideas burguesas

RESURGIR

Superrealismo

Expresionismo

mediocre

arquitectura

ideas liberales

Modernismo

joven

movimiento

estilo

REVOLUCIONAR

DAR surpresas

SACAR notas

carrera

arquitecto

centro

PEOPLE

calderero

Antoni Gaudí

artista

miembro

originario

Sociedad/ciudad

Reus (Gerona)

conciudadanos

Barcelona

familia

PLACE

101

TABLE 11	SPANISH TEXT: EXAMPLES OF SEMANTIC NETWORKS				
	makes things	helps people	creative	self-employed	accepted member of society
arquitecto	sí		sí	sí	sí
artista	sí		sí	sí	?
calderero	sí			sí	no
carpintero	sí		sí		sí
medico		sí		sí	sí
policía		sí			sí

TABLE 12	SPANISH TEXT: EXAMPLES OF COLLOCATION POSSIBILITIES (X for subject, Y for object)			
	ser humilde	revolu-cionar	resurgir	ser el precursor
arquitecto		X		X
calderero	X			
movimiento		a Y	X	de un Y
sociedad		a Y		
familia	X			
cultura		a Y	X	

TABLE 13	**FRENCH EXAMPLE: ARRANGEMENT OF VOCABULARY TO PRODUCE TELEGRAPHIC TEXT**			

Qui?	Quoi?	Où?	Quand?	Comment?
	incendie ravager	Besançon bâtiment	En avril 1985	
gamins	jouer	cage d'escalier		habituellement
	fumée épaisse envahir	cage d'escalier		
C.Tournier et deux autres habitants	pénétrer	immeuble		
	frayer un passage	->trappe de secours		
	trappe de secours condamnée			
Camille Tournier	pénétrer	->appartement		
pompiers	évacuer 27 enfants			échelle
C.T.	intoxiqué			fumée épaisse
	coeur faiblissant			
	hospitalisé			
	opération			
	perdre emploi			

TABLE 14	GERMAN EXAMPLE: ARRANGEMENT OF VOCABULARY TO PRODUCE TELEGRAPHIC TEXT			
Wer?	**Was?**	**Wo?**	**Wann?**	**Wie?**
Gerda und Erika Zwillinge	geboren	Berlin-Karlshorst	7 Juli 1939	
Gerda	kommen	-> Kranken-haus	1943. während der Bomben-nächte	mit Lungen-entzündung
Gerda	4 Jahre alt.			
Gerda	evakuiert	-> Leipzig	eines Nachts	mit allen anderen Patienten.
Gerda	Namens-bändchen verlieren	beim Transport		
Gerda	kommen	-> Waisen-haus in Leipzig		
Gerda	kommen	-> Pflege-familie	später	
Gerda	ziehen	->ₜ Augsburg	1978	
Erika	bleiben	Berlin		
Eltern	Gerda suchen		1943 Jahrelang	mit Hilfe des Roten Kreuzes.

TABLE 15   **SPANISH EXAMPLE: ARRANGEMENT OF VOCABULARY TO PRODUCE TELEGRAPHIC TEXT**

From the first cluster (Figure 8) we get:

¿Quién?	¿Qué?	¿Dónde?	¿Cuándo?	¿Cómo?
anciano despistado	atro-pellar	Plaza de Cataluña, Barcelona	el 7 de junio de 1926	por un tranvía
	conducir	-> hospital		
nadie	conocer			
	ident-ificar		dos días después	
A. Gaudí	morir		poco después	

From the second cluster (Figure 9) we get:

¿Quién?	¿Qué?	¿Dónde?	¿Cuándo?	¿Cómo?
A. Gaudí Arquitecto	revolucionar a la sociedad catalana			artísticamente
El joven Gaudí	comenzar a dar sorpresas a sus conciudadanos		último cuarto del siglo XIX.	
	sacar notas bastante mediocres		en su carrera de arquitectura.	

We have stressed above the importance of the sound of words in their citation form for storage and access in memory. A practical way of providing this is to have on tape a native speaker's presentation of how he allocated the words to different clusters: "In the PEOPLE set I put *crow, fox*, and *specialist*. I put *gourmet* and *epicure* in the intersection of PEOPLE and EVENT ..." and so on. This give learners a reason for listening to words in lists as they compare their clusters with those created by the native speaker.

(iii) Development of discourse: creating a telegraphic text

With clusters and grids of the kind illustrated in Figures 3-9 and Tables 4-12, learners have the materials from which to create telegraphic texts. This might best be done by laying out the information from the clusters in linear form, with headings that match the focal points of the sets: WHO?, WHAT?, WHERE?, WHEN?, HOW?. Tables 13-15 offer examples of what this process might yield when applied to our sample texts in French, German and Spanish. In the case of the Spanish text it might be worth constructing a profile of Antoni Gaudí as follows:

Nombre	Gaudí
Ciudad di origen:	Reus (Gerona)
Familia	Caldereros
Carrera	Arquitecto
Vestido	modestamente
Documentación	ninguna

(iv) Developing syntax at sentence level

Learners can now use this material as the basis for constructing their own text. If they have used Post-its as suggested, they simply transfer the elements of each sentence to another page and order them as appropriate, making whatever morpho-syntactic changes are necessary. Morpho-syntax (2a in Table 2) is crucial at this stage, and the use of Post-its allows learners to concentrate exclusively on this component.   At this stage they will require input that provides them with the relevant morpho-syntactic information. Giving them a simplified version of the original text that uses the key words already provided can be an effective way of doing this - verbs are presented in their correct forms, adjectives agree with nouns, the word order is correct, and so on. However, the straightforward provision of a simplified text is less likely to be of value than a jumbled version of the same simplified text. Unscrambling the text requires learners to use their world and discourse knowledge; at the same time, they construct a "schema" or "script" which will create space for language processing when they are given the original authentic text.

Once again a useful addition here would be the provision of the correct sequence of the simplified text on tape, which enables the learners to listen with a purpose, comparing their sequence to that on the tape and at the same time becoming familiar with the vocabulary in context.

By way of illustration we give only the first few sentences of texts that might be created for this kind of use. (Incidentally, learners' texts often diverge quite markedly from the original and from one another in content. It is important to consider their texts as creations which have value in their own right. As they are edited on the basis of comparison with the simplified and authentic versions they may even develop to the point where they can be used as reading material for other learners.)

Simplified texts as sources of morpho-syntactic information

Unscrambling a text activates "schemata" and "scripts"

Using audio recordings to give practice in listening with a purpose

Examples of possible simplified texts

French text

Simplified French text

Un incendie a ravagé un bâtiment à Besançon en avril 1985.
Des gamins jouaient dans une cage d'escalier.
Les gamins ont été bloqués par le feu.
Camille Tournier a pénétré dans les couloirs du bâtiment et a frayé un chemin jusqu'à la cage d'escalier.

German text

Simplified German text

Die Zwillinge Gerda und Erika wurden am 7 Juli 1939 in Berlin-Karlshorst geboren.
1943 kam Gerda mit Lungenentzündung ins Krankenhaus.

Eines Nachts wurde sie mit allen anderen Patienten nach Leipzig evakuiert.

Spanish text

El 7 de junio de 1926 un anciano despistado es atropellado por un tranvía junto a la Plaza de Cataluña en Barcelona.
X conduce el anciano a un hospital.
Nadie conoce al anciano.
Dos dias después identifican al anciano.
Es Antonio Gaudí, arquitecto famoso.
Muere poco después.
Ha revolucionado artísticamente a la sociedad catalana.

Simplified Spanish text

Cloze exercises again: French example

At this stage cloze exercises can again be employed as in the example below, based on the French text. The advantages of this approach should be obvious: learners have more confidence in using vocabulary which they are by now familiar with; and it helps them to focus on morpho-syntax at sentence level in a meaningful way.

Un incendie a (1)_____ un bâtiment à Besançon en avril 1985.
Des gamins jouaient dans une cage d'escalier.
Les gamins ont été bloqués par le feu.
Camille Tournier a pénétré dans les (2)_____ du bâtiment et a (3)_____ un chemin jusqu'à la cage d'escalier.

(v) Developing syntax above sentence level

Developing a fully coherent and cohesive text

The final task in our exercise chain is to develop a fully coherent and cohesive text. There are frequently different possibilities at this point, as the French example shows. The authentic text that has been the source of the exercise chain can be used to correct and edit learners' texts, and this offers further opportunities for developing a deliberately analytical approach to words in context.

French text

French example

Possibility 1
En avril 1985 Camille Tournier a pénétré dans les couloirs d'un bâtiment à Besançon ravagé par un incendie où des

108

gamins jouaient dans une cage d'escalier.

Possibility 2
En avril 1985, alors qu'un incendie ravageait son immeuble à Besançon, Camille Tournier a pénétré dans les
couloirs (pour sauver) des gamins qui jouaient dans une
cage d'escalier.

German
example

German text
Die Zwillinge Gerda und Erika wurden am 7. Juli 1939 in
Berlin-Karlshorst geboren. Gerda war 4 Jahre alt als sie
mit Lungenentzündung ins Krankenhaus kam.

Spanish
example

Spanish text
El 7 de junio de 1926 un anciano despistado es atropellado por un tranvía junto a la Plaza de Cataluña en Barcelona. Se lo conduce a un hospital, donde nadie lo conoce. Dos días después le identifican, pero muere poco
después.

A variant of the
foregoing chain
of exercises:
information
exchange via
role play

We began this chain of exercises with word clusters and
noted that in all three texts there might be more than one
cluster. An interesting variant might be to divide the class
into two groups and have each group work on separate
sections of the text. This means that each group would end
up with part of the information communicated by the text as
a whole, yet that part would be quite coherent. Information
might be exchanged at the end of the chain of exercises
through a role play exercise, such as a court-case for the
French text, or an interview for the German and Spanish
texts. Productive oral work of this kind will have first-order
authenticity since real information will be exchanged and
reactions to the information elicited.

4.7 Conclusion

Putting
authentic texts
at the centre
of language
teaching

At present most teachers use authentic texts to supple-
ment a language course book. However, the arguments that
we elaborated in Chapters 1 and 2 carry the implication that
authentic texts should be the centre around which all other
language learning materials are organized. Authentik has
plans to develop various kinds of support material for both

teacher and learner that should make this easier to achieve; but in the meantime teachers who want to construct their course on authentic texts must assume a considerable burden of organization.

Any attempt to implement the pedagogical techniques that we have presented in Chapters 3 and 4 must take account of the practical constraints that impose themselves on every course of language teaching. To begin with there are the constraints that arise from the educational system. First language acquisition is a highly intensive process that engages the child for a large proportion of its waking hours; and the difference between first and "naturalistic" second language acquisition lies less in the intensity of the process than in the fact that the second language learner may be able to withdraw between times to a first language environment, for example by returning to his family at the end of the working day. By contrast, foreign language teaching in formal educational environments is traditionally a matter of very small doses administered over a relatively long period. This must create difficulties for the activation of natural acquisition processes, and it challenges teachers to use all their ingenuity to keep learners' attention focussed on the target language. No doubt the question of a more intensive approach to language teaching should be at the centre of any thoroughgoing overhaul of the second-level curriculum; but in the meantime teachers have to find ways of coping with the situation as it is. Many of the activities we have been concerned with in Chapters 3 and 4 not only require time in their own right but also lead naturally into further activities, and it is difficult to maintain momentum if every lesson comes to an end after forty minutes. Some teachers may be able to counteract this to the extent of arranging for each of their classes to have at least one double period each week. The choice of homework activities is also crucial in maintaining continuity.

The learners themselves are a second source of constraints. Even supposing that our classes are composed of learners with a higher than average level of interest who present no discipline problems, we still face the fact that the

Constraints imposed by the educational system

The problem of insufficient intensiveness

Limitations imposed by the length of lessons

Homework and continuity

Constraints that arise from the learners

attention span of even the most committed learners is limited: there is always the risk that boredom will set in before they get to the end of a particular activity. It is specially important to bear this in mind when learners are being led through a chain of activities based on a single authentic text. The people who devised the chain were no doubt sustained by the challenge that this process made to their ingenuity, and it probably never occurred to them that learners could become bored long before reaching the end

of the chain. In general learners are more likely to succeed if they have a clear sense of purpose which enables them to organize their thoughts and learning activities efficiently. This is another reason why they should be encouraged to become as autonomous as the systems permits.

Constraints
arising from
teachers'
limited
preparation
time ...

Further constraints arise from the teacher's limited preparation time. It is one thing to understand the principles on which an exercise is based, but quite another to find the time to devise quantitities of exercises sufficient to keep a class of thirty learners occupied for four lessons a week throughout the school year. No doubt this is why most teachers use ready-made exercises. However, one of the central convictions of this book is that the most effective language learning may be based not on exercises that take hours to devise and minutes to do, but rather on activities that take very little time at all to prepare but quite a long

time to perform. Also, as we have suggested at various points in Chapters 3 and 4, learners may usefully devise and correct exercises for one another. This is especially the case with exercises that are focussed on vocabulary and grammar. An authentic text can rapidly be turned into various kinds of cloze exercise. For example, whole words can be deleted in order to raise issues of synonymy, antonymy and collocation; alternatively, the inflexional system can be brought into focus by deleting only inflexional endings. Learners can also set one another exercises that involve the rewriting of authentic texts: a third-person text can be transposed into the first person and vice versa; or a text written in the past can be transposed to the present. Finally, learners can discover much about the syntax of their target language by reducing the sentences of an authentic text to their component propositions and then combining simple declarative propositions into new compound sentences.

The biggest constraint of all: public examinations

But perhaps the biggest single constraint that teachers feel is the one imposed by the public examinations. Objections to pedagogical innovation frequently take the form: "That's all well and good in theory, but it's nothing like the exam my learners have to pass." We have seen, however, that this need not necessarily be true. Activities of the type suggested in this book develop the underlying components of the skills required for examinations. The analysis of the text types and tasks set in public examinations presented in the appendix is intended to provide a benchmark against which to measure the value and effectiveness of what is proposed here.

Suggestions for further reading

Readers interested in finding out more about recent work on vocabulary should consult *Vocabulary: Applied Linguistic Perspectives*, by R. Carter (London: Allen & Unwin; 1987) or *Vocabulary and Language Teaching*, edited by R. Carter and M. McCarthy (London: Longman; 1988).

W. Rutherford and M. Sharwood Smith have edited a useful collection of readings on different aspects of grammar in language teaching: *Grammar and Second Language Teaching* (Rowley, Mass.: Newbury House; 1987). *Grammar in Action*, by C. Frank and M. Rinvolucri (London: Prentice Hall International; 1987) and *Teaching Grammar*, by S. McKay (London: Prentice Hall International; 1987) are a useful source of practical suggestions for contextualized grammar work.

Interactive Approaches to Second Language Reading, edited by P. Carrell, J. Devine and D. Eskey (Cambridge University Press; 1988) contains some articles that elaborate theories of reading; while *Learning to Write: First Language/Second Language*, edited by A. Freedman, I. Pringle and J. Yalden (London & New York: Longman; 1983) approaches the development of writing skills from a number of different perspectives.

F. Grellet's *Developing Reading Skills: a Practical Guide to Reading Comprehension* (Cambridge University Press; 1981) and C. Nuttall's *Teaching Reading Skills in a Foreign Language* (London: Heinemann; 1982) contain many practical suggestions for developing skills in reading.

Appendix
Public examinations in the United Kingdom

This appendix analyses the public examinations in modern languages in the United Kingdom in terms of the different text types and tasks that are used. In the first section, which deals with GCSE, we have based our analysis on sample papers from three examination boards and have also included an analysis of the Scottish Certificate of Education Standard Grade. In the second section, which analyses the new A-Level examinations, we have used papers from five examination boards in England. In this section we have also included the Scottish Certificate of Education Higher Grade and the Certificate of Sixth Year Studies. We have confined our analysis in all cases to the reading and writing components of the examinations.

Each examination board publishes its own syllabus, setting out comprehensively the aims, content, assessment objectives and techniques for the different levels. Detailed marking schemes are also provided. This makes examination requirements much clearer than heretofore, and incidentally facilitates the task of analysis. Most if not all examination boards now use positive marking, which means that candidates are given credit for what they get right and also that the full range of marks is now available.

1 GCSE and SCE Standard Grade Examinations

In the GCSE examinations there are two levels, Basic and Higher, while the Scottish examinations have three levels: Foundation, General and Credit.

The first point to be made is that in these examinations the traditional division between the "four skills" (listening, speaking, reading and writing) tends to be rigorously maintained. This explains why all comprehension questions and all instructions are in the mother tongue. However, some of the tasks used to test the writing skill require candidates to respond to texts in the target language, which obviously demands comprehension as well as production of the target language. The second point to be made is that all the texts used are authentic, though they are not always presented in their original format. Thirdly, we found in all examinations that while the types of texts used were quite varied, the kinds of task candidates were required to perform were quite limited. Thus there were only two kinds of comprehension task: (a) basic comprehension of facts, and (b) comprehension of how facts relate to one another in a text ("the ability to identify important points or themes within an extended piece of writing and to draw conclusions from, and see relations within, an extended text" - Northern Ireland Syllabus for GCSE Examination 1989, p.315). We identified two types of writing task: responding to a text in the target language, and writing according to instructions given in the mother tongue.

Table A1 provides an overview of the text types and reading and writing tasks used by the different examination boards whose papers we have analysed. No distinction is made for the different languages, which means that the table may show more text types than occur on one paper. The text types used fall into six general categories: (i) public notices, (ii) instructions (for games, recipes, etc.), (iii) tourist guides, (iv) messages to individuals, (v) articles from the media, (vi) fiction (usually narrative, with or without dialogue). However, for p rposes of analysis it proved helpful to subdivide categories (i), (iv) and (v).

TABLE A1   **OVERVIEW OF TEXT TYPES AND TASKS USED IN GCSE AND RELATED EXAMINATIONS**

TEXT TYPES

P1	Signs
P2	Advertisements
P3	Timetables, notices, menus
I	Instructions (games, recipes etc)
T	Tourist guides, brochures
M1	Notes, messages, postcards, lists, diary entries
M2	Letters
A1	Weather reports
A2	Reports of news, human interest, etc
A3	Interviews with "personalities"
A4	Argumentative articles, commentaries etc
A5	Horoscopes
F	Fictional narrative including dialogue

TASKS

Comp1	Comprehension of basic facts
Comp2	Comprehension of relationships between facts etc
Write1	Writing according to instructions given in English or describing a set of pictures
Write2	Writing in response to target language text

TABLE A1 CONTINUED

	P1	P2	P3	I	T	M1	M2	A1	A2	A3	A4	A5	F
Scotland													
Foundation													
Comp1		x	x	x					x				
Comp2		x	x										
General													
Comp1		x	x	x	x	x	x				x		
Comp2		x	x	x							x		
Write 1 (optional)						x	x						
Credit													
Comp1		x		x			x		x	x	x		
Comp2		x		x			x		x	x	x		
Write2 (optional)											x		
London and East Anglian Group													
Basic													
Comp1	x	x	x		x		x						
Comp2		x											
Write1							x						x
Write2						x	x						
Higher													
Comp1		x							x	x	x		
Comp2		x							x	x	x	x	
Write1							x		x				
Write2									x				

116

TABLE A1 CONTINUED

	P1	P2	P3	I	T	M1	M2	A1	A2	A3	A4	A5	F
Midland Examining Board													
Basic													
Comp1	x	x	x	x			x						
Comp2													
Write1					x								
Higher													
Comp1		x				x	x		x	x			
Comp2		x				x	x		x	x			
Write1						x			x	x			x
Northern Ireland													
Basic													
Comp1	x	x	x			x	x		x				
Comp2													
Write1					x	x	x						
(Higher)													
Comp1		x	x			x	x						x
Comp2		x	x			x	x						x
Write1						x			x				

Table A1 allows us to make two general points. First, it is rather surprising that newspaper reports containing basic narratives figure so little. Such reports are often understandable by learners at quite an early stage, and they offer much more material for language learning than some of the public notice texts. Secondly, it is not always the case that what candidates are required to write corresponds to the type of text to which they have been accustomed in their reading. For example, the picture essay is a feature of some examinations which do not test comprehension of narrative texts.

The analysis of the examination papers threw up some other interesting points which are not obvious from Table A1. Sometimes the visual support provided with texts made the task of comprehension much easier. There was, for example, one instance where candidates had to answer questions relating to instructions for a board game where a picture of the board itself greatly facilitated the task. In other cases the visual material accompanying texts was unhelpful, even distracting.

There is also the question of the authenticity of presentation. In some cases texts were given in their authentic format, and in others they were not. As a general principle we would advocate the use of authentic format; however, it must be said that the handwriting in some of the letters and notes was not always easy to decipher. This could add to the difficulty of comprehension.

Finally, it was interesting to note that quite a high proportion of the basic comprehension tasks could have been performed with no more than a knowledge of key words. This underlines our basic contention that vocabulary is perhaps the key element in language acquisition. In a few cases world knowledge would have helped some candidates. Again this adds support to the argument in the main body of the book which stresses the importance of training learners to use all their resources in trying to come to an understanding of texts.

2 A-Level

At this level it was remarkable that the text types used in the examinations analysed were quite limited, while the tasks to be performed covered a much wider range than in the GCSE exams. The texts were mainly either journalistic/evaluative or narrative (with or without dialogue).

We have seen that in the the GCSE exams the distinction between the four skills was rigorously maintained. By contrast, at this level skills were often integrated, at least to some extent. For example, some examination boards tested reading and writing skills in the same paper, and all the papers we analysed contained at least some mix of reading and writing. However, in some cases candidates were required to answer comprehension questions in English; these are marked with a subscript "e" in Table A2. Since there is a continuum at this level between reading and writing activities, with some tasks clearly involving both reading and writing in the target language, we have decided not to make a clear-cut distinction between them.

At this level comprehension invariably involves more than mere understanding of the facts; a candidate must be able to get the main points but also to see relationships between different facts. We have therefore grouped all tasks involving this type of comprehension under one heading in Table A2. Some comprehension tasks involve appreciating the writer's viewpoint or attitude; these have been grouped under the heading of appreciation.

Another component of the A-Level examinations is the civilization/culture/literature of the target language community. This component is variously treated by the different examination boards, and we have not been able to include all the approaches to examining it in our analysis.

Finally, as for the GCSE analysis, we make no distinction between languages, so that not all the tasks listed for a particular examination board need have appeared on one examination paper. Also, in some cases more than one input text is used as the basis for one or more tasks to be performed.

TABLE A2 **OVERVIEW OF TEXT TYPES AND TASKS USED IN A-LEVEL AND RELATED EXAMINATIONS**

TASKS

Com	Comprehension
Ap	Appreciation of viewpoints etc
Su	Summary
T1	Translation into English
T2	Translation into target language
Cl	Cloze
Vo	Vocabulary tests
Re	Response to text (evaluative comment, narrative etc.)
L	Letter in response to text
E	Essay

Tasks:	Com	Ap	Su	T1	T2	Cl	Vo	Re	L	E
Examination Board and input text types										
AEB										
Journalistic	X_e			X				X		
Narrative	X_e									
Eng.text	X				X					
Civilization										
Set topics										X
JMB										
Journalistic	X	X	X	X	X	X	X	X	X	X
Narrative				X	X					
No input text										X
Literature										
Set texts		X								X_e

119

TABLE A2 CONTINUED

Tasks:	Com	Ap	Su	T1	T2	Cl	Vo	Re	L	E
Examination Board and input text types.										
Univ.of Cambridge L.Ex.Synd.										
Journalistic	X	X	X				X			
Narrative	X	X	X							
Eng.text	X		X							
Thematic studies										
Set texts		X								X
Oxford & Cambridge										
Journalistic			X	X	X	X	X			
Letter related to above text									X	
Reported Interview	X_e			X						
Literary txt				X	X					
No input txt										X
Civilization Set topics		X_e								X_e
University of London										
Narrative				X						
Interview	X									
Journalistic text in Eng					X					
Advertisement										X
Civilization texts on set topics		X						X		X
Literature set texts		X_e								X_e

TABLE A2 CONTINUED

Tasks:	Com	Ap	Su	T1	T2	Cl	Vo	Re	L	E
Examination Board and input text types.										
Scotland Higher Grade										
Interview	X	X		X			X			
Advertisement								X	X	
Narrative								X		
Horoscope								X		
Letter						X				
Narrative						X				
Certificate of Sixth Year Studies										
Journalistic Literary	X	X		X			X			
Verse		X								
Narrative		X								
No input text										X

Perhaps the most interesting feature of the new examinations is that one or two texts often form the basis of a whole series of tasks. In one case, for example, a cloze test had to be performed on a paragraph following the main text, and a paragraph in English on the same topic was used for translation into the target language. This allowed candidates to concentrate on the mechanisms of the language, since the vocabulary they needed was already available in the input texts. In another case candidates had to use general information from one text in order to prepare a response to specific requests in a letter. This new approach involves students in using language much more meaningfully than in older style examinations.

We have discussed cloze tests in the main body of the book. In one of the examples found in A-level examinations the words were given, in their correct form, but some extra words were included over and above. This is an interesting variant of the standard cloze test. In the Scottish Higher Grade the cloze test is a completely separate paper.

Finally, it is interesting to note that three of the five boards put quite a lot of emphasis on vocabulary knowledge, with candidates having to find equivalents for words or phrases found in the text. The Scottish Higher Grade uses the interesting variant of giving two dictionary definitions of words and asking the student to choose the appropriate one for the context.